# WASHINGTON
## *and* OREGON
# NATURE GUIDE

*Erin McCloskey*

with contributions from Andy Bezener,
Krista Kagume & Linda Kershaw

LONE
PINE

Lone Pine Publishing International

**Distributed by Lone Pine Publishing**
1808 B Street NW, Suite 140
Auburn, WA, USA  98001

**Website:** www.lonepinepublishing.com

**Publisher's Cataloging-In-Publication Data**
(Prepared by The Donohue Group, Inc.)

McCloskey, Erin, 1970–
  Washington & Oregon nature guide / Erin McCloskey.

     p. : col. ill., col. maps ;  cm.

  Includes bibliographical references and index.
  ISBN-13: 978-976-8200-43-3
  ISBN-10: 976-8200-43-X

1. Natural history—Washington (State)—Guidebooks.   2. Natural history—Oregon—Guidebooks.   3. Washington (State)—Guidebooks.   4. Oregon—Guidebooks.   I. Title.   II. Title: Washington and Oregon nature guide

QH105.W2 M33 2008
508.7/97

*Cover Illustrations:* Frank Burman, Ted Nordhagen, Gary Ross, Ian Sheldon
*Illustrations:* Frank Burman, Ivan Droujinin, Kindrie Grove, Linda Kershaw, Ted Nordhagen, George Penetrante, Gary Ross, Ian Sheldon
A complete list of illustration credits appears on p. 4.

**Disclaimer:** This guide is not intended to be a "how to" reference guide for food or medicinal uses of plants. We do not recommend experimentation by readers, and we caution that a number of woody plants in Washington and Oregon, including some used traditionally as medicines, are poisonous and harmful.

PC: 15

# TABLE OF CONTENTS

# ILLUSTRATION CREDITS

**Frank Burman:** 157, 163, 187, 188, 190, 195, 159a, 159b, 160c, 160d, 162a, 165d, 165e, 166a, 166b, 166d, 167a, 167b, 170b, 170c, 171d, 172b, 174c, 175a, 175c, 176a, 177a, 177b, 179c, 182c, 183a, 184b, 184c, 185b, 185c, 186b, 186c, 189a, 189c, 191a, 191b, 192a, 192b, 193b, 194c, 194d, 194e, 196a, 197b, 197c, 198c, 199a, 199c, 200a, 201b, 201c, 202a

**Ivan Droujinin:** 122a, 127a, 127c, 153c

**Kindrie Grove:** 71a

**Ted Nordhagen:** 89b, 93b, 94a, 95, 96a, 97a, 97b, 98b, 120, 101c, 102a, 104b, 104c, 105a, 105c, 106c, 107a, 107c, 108a, 108b, 109a, 109b, 110b, 111b, 111c, 113b, 113c, 114a, 114b, 115a, 117a, 117c, 118b, 119b, 119c

**George Penetrante:** 134b, 134c, 135b

**Gary Ross:** 48, 49, 50, 51, 52, 53, 54, 55, 56, 57, 62b, 63b, 64, 65, 66, 67, 68, 69, 70, 71b, 71c, 72, 73, 74, 75, 76, 77, 78, 79, 82, 83, 84, 85, 86, 87, 88, 89a, 89c, 90, 91, 92, 93a, 93c, 94b, 94c, 96b, 96c, 97c, 98a, 98c, 99, 100, 103, 112, 116, 124, 124, 125, 125, 126, 129, 130, 101a, 101b, 102b, 104a, 105b, 106a, 106b, 107b, 108c, 109c, 110a, 110c, 111a, 113a, 114c, 115b, 115c, 117b, 118a, 118c, 119a, 122b, 127b, 128a, 128c

**Ian Sheldon:** 58, 59, 60, 61, 62a, 63a, 123, 128b, 132, 133, 134a, 135a, 138, 139, 140, 141, 142, 143, 144, 145, 146, 147, 148, 149, 150, 151, 152, 153a, 153b, 158, 159d, 160b, 161, 162b, 162c, 162d, 164, 165a, 165b, 165c, 166c, 167c, 169, 170a, 170d, 170e, 171a, 171b, 171c, 172a, 172c, 172d, 173, 174a, 174b, 174d, 175b, 176b, 176c, 177c, 177d, 178, 179a, 179b, 182a, 182b, 183b, 183c, 184a, 185a, 186a, 189b, 191c, 192c, 193a, 193c, 193d, 194a, 194b, 196b, 196c, 197a, 198a, 198b, 199b, 200b, 200c, 201a, 202b, 202c, 203

# ACKNOWLEDGMENTS

The publisher and author thank Tamara Eder and Krista Kagume for their previous work on the mammals and birds research and to all the authors of former Lone Pine texts who have created such a great library of background information. Thanks to Andy Bezener and Linda Kershaw for their work on the first of this nature guide series, the *Rocky Mountain Nature Guide*.

Special thanks to the following people for their assistance in the development of the species lists: Ian Sheldon (author and illustrator of *Seashore Guide of the Pacific Northwest* and *Bugs of Washington and Oregon*), Maddalena Bearzi, PhD (president and co-founder of the Ocean Conservation Society), Robert Steelquist (sanctuary education coordinator for the National Oceanic and Atmospheric Administration), Damian Fagan (director of the Central Oregon Audubon Society), William L. McArthur, PhD (regional silviculturist, USDA Forest Service) and Margaret Kain (assistant director NR, Forest Products and Vegetation, Pacific Northwest Region, USDA Forest Service).

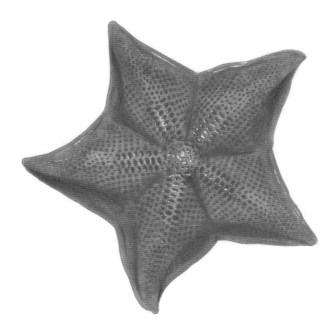

**MAMMALS**

Mountain Goat
p. 48

Bighorn Sheep
p. 48

Pronghorn
p. 49

Elk
p. 49

Mule Deer
p. 50

White-tailed Deer
p. 50

Moose
p. 51

Caribou
p. 51

Feral Horse
p. 52

Feral Pig
p. 52

Mountain Lion
p. 53

Canada Lynx
p. 53

Bobcat
p. 54

American Black Bear
p. 54

Grizzly Bear
p. 55

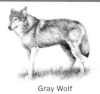

Gray Wolf
p.55

Coyote
p. 56

Gray Fox
p. 56

Kit Fox
p. 57

Red Fox
p. 57

Gray Whale
p. 58

Minke Whale
p. 58

Fin Whale
p. 59

Humpback Whale
p. 59

Orca
p. 60

Short-beaked Common Dolphin
p. 60

Risso's Dolphin
p. 61

Pacific White-sided Doilphin
p. 61

Northern Elephant Seal
p. 62

Harbor Seal
p. 62

Northern Sea-Lion
p. 63

Sea Otter
p. 63

Northern River Otter
p. 64

American Marten
p. 64

Fisher
p. 64

Short-tailed Weasel
p. 65

Long-tailed Weasel
p. 65

American Mink
p. 65

Wolverine
p. 66

American Badger
p. 66

**Striped Skunk**
p. 66

**Western Spotted Skunk**
p. 67

**Ringtail**
p. 67

**Northern Raccoon**
p. 67

**Porcupine**
p. 68

**Mountain Beaver**
p. 68

**Beaver**
p. 68

**Nutria**
p. 69

**Common Muskrat**
p. 69

**Bushy-tailed Woodrat**
p. 69

**Norway Rat**
p. 70

**Deer Mouse**
p. 70

**House Mouse**
p. 70

**Montane Vole**
p. 71

**Pacific Jumping Mouse**
p. 71

**Great Basin Pocket Mouse**
p. 71

**Ord's Kangaroo Rat**
p. 72

**Northern Pocket Gopher**
p. 72

**Townsend's Chipmunk**
p. 72

**Yellow-bellied Marmot**
p. 73

**Golden-mantled Ground Squirrel**
p. 73

**Western Gray Squirrel**
p. 73

**Douglas's Squirrel**
p. 74

**Northern Flying Squirrel**
p. 74

Pygmy Rabbit
p. 74

Brush Rabbit
p. 75

Mountain Cottontail
p. 75

Snowshoe Hare
p. 75

White-tailed Jackrabbit
p. 76

Pika
p. 76

Little Brown Bat
p. 76

Hoary Bat
p. 77

Silver-haired Bat
p. 77

Big Brown Bat
p. 77

Western Pipistrelle
p. 78

Townsend's Big-eared Bat
p. 78

Coast Mole
p. 78

Vagrant Shrew
p. 79

Virginia Opossum
p. 79

Canada Goose
p. 82

Tundra Swan
p. 82

Wood Duck
p. 83

Gadwall
p. 83

Mallard
p. 84

Northern Pintail
p. 84

Green-winged Teal
p. 85

Ring-necked Duck
p. 85

Lesser Scaup
p. 86

Surf Scoter
p. 86

Common Goldeneye
p. 87

Common Merganser
p. 87

Ring-necked Pheasant
p. 88

Ruffed Grouse
p. 88

California Quail
p. 88

Common Loon
p. 89

Eared Grebe
p. 89

American White Pelican
p. 89

Double-crested Cormorant
p. 90

Great Blue Heron
p. 90

Black-crowned Night-Heron
p. 90

Turkey Vulture
p. 91

Osprey
p. 91

Bald Eagle
p. 91

Northern Harrier
p. 92

Sharp-shinned Hawk
p. 92

Red-tailed Hawk
p. 92

Rough-legged Hawk
p. 93

**BIRDS**

American Kestrel
p. 93

Peregrine Falcon
p. 93

Sora
p. 94

Sandhill Crane
p. 94

Black-bellied Plover
p. 94

Snowy Plover
p. 95

Killdeer
p. 95

Black Oystercatcher
p. 95

American Avocet
p. 96

Spotted Sandpiper
p. 96

Greater Yellowlegs
p. 96

Long-billed Curlew
p. 97

Black Turnstone
p. 97

Western Sandpiper
p. 97

Dunlin
p. 98

Long-billed Dowitcher
p. 98

Wilson's Snipe
p. 98

Bonaparte's Gull
p. 99

Ring-billed Gull
p. 99

Western Gull
p. 99

Caspian Tern
p. 100

Common Murre
p. 100

Marbled Murrelet
p. 100

Tufted Puffin
p. 101

11

**BIRDS**

Rock Pigeon
p. 101

Mourning Dove
p. 101

Western Screech-Owl
p. 102

Great Horned Owl
p. 102

Burrowing Owl
p. 103

Spotted Owl
p. 103

Common Nighthawk
p. 104

Vaux's Swift
p. 104

Anna's Hummingbird
p. 104

Rufous Hummingbird
p. 105

Belted Kingfisher
p. 105

Lewis's Woodpecker
p. 105

Downy Woodpecker
p. 106

Northern Flicker
p. 106

Olive-sided Flycatcher
p. 106

Western Wood-Pewee
p. 107

Pacific-slope Flycatcher
p. 107

Western Kingbird
p. 107

Northern Shrike
p. 108

Warbling Vireo
p. 108

Steller's Jay
p. 108

Clark's Nutcracker
p. 109

Black-billed Magpie
p. 109

American Crow
p. 109

Common Raven
p. 110

Horned Lark
p. 110

Violet-green Swallow
p. 110

Black-capped Chickadee
p. 111

Bushtit
p. 111

Red-breasted Nuthatch
p. 111

House Wren
p. 112

Winter Wren
p. 112

American Dipper
p. 112

Golden-crowned Kinglet
p. 113

American Robin
p. 113

Wrentit
p. 113

European Starling
p. 114

Cedar Waxwing
p. 114

Orange-crowned Warbler
p. 114

Yellow-rumped Warbler
p. 115

Black-throated Gray Warbler
p. 115

Townsend's Warbler
p. 115

Wilson's Warbler
p. 116

Western Tanager
p. 116

Spotted Towhee
p. 116

Chipping Sparrow
p. 117

Song Sparrow
p. 117

White-crowned Sparrow
p. 117

**BIRDS**

Dark-eyed Junco
p. 118

Black-headed Grosbeak
p. 118

Red-winged Blackbird
p. 118

Western Meadowlark
p. 119

House Finch
p. 119

Pine Siskin
p. 119

American Goldfinch
p. 120

House Sparrow
p. 120

**AMPHIBIANS & REPTILES**

California Newt
p. 122

Long-toed Salamander
p. 122

Coastal Giant Salamander
p. 123

Van Dyke's Salamander
p. 123

Great Basin Spadefoot
p. 124

Western Toad
p. 124

Coastal Tailed Frog
p. 124

Bullfrog
p. 125

Red-legged Frog
p. 125

Pacific Treefrog
p. 125

Western Pond Turtle
p. 126

Painted Turtle
p. 126

Sagebrush Lizard
p. 127

Western Fence Lizard
p. 127

Common Side-blotched Lizard
p. 127

Pygmy Short-horned Lizard
p. 128

Western Skink
p. 128

Northern Alligator Lizard
p. 128

Rubber Boa
p. 129

Yellow-bellied Racer
p. 129

Ring-necked Snake
p. 129

Gophersnake
p. 130

Common Gartersnake
p. 130

Western Rattlesnake
p. 130

Chinook Salmon
p. 132

Cutthroat Trout
p. 132

Rainbow Trout
p. 132

Brook Trout
p. 133

Brown Trout
p. 133

Black Prickleback
p. 133

**FISH**

Blackeye Goby
p. 134

Blue Rockfish
p. 134

Lingcod
p. 134

Tidepool Sculpin
p. 135

Pacific Sanddab
p. 135

**INVERTEBRATES**

Black Tegula
p. 138

Lewis' Moon Snail
p. 138

Pacific Razor Clam
p. 138

California Mussel
p. 139

Gumboot Chiton
p. 139

Lined Chiton
p. 139

Sea Lemon
p. 140

Red Sea Cucumber
p. 140

Bat Star
p. 140

Ochre Sea Star
p. 141

Eccentric Sand Dollar
p. 141

Purple Sea Urchin
p. 141

Aggregating Anemone
p. 142

Giant Green Anemone
p. 142

Orange Cup Coral
p. 142

Purple Sponge
p. 143

Moon Jellyfish
p. 143

Red Octopus
p. 143

Giant Acorn Barnacle
p. 144

Barred Shrimp
p. 144

Dungeness Crab
p. 144

Purple Shore Crab
p. 145

Blue-handed Hermit Crab
p. 145

Western Tiger Swallowtail
p. 146

Spring Azure
p. 146

Clouded Sulphur
p. 146

Orange Sulphur
p. 146

Pacific Fritillary
p. 147

Mourning Cloak
p. 147

Polyphemus Moth
p. 147

Common Spreadwing
p. 148

Green Darner
p. 148

American Emerald
p. 148

Common Whitetail
p. 149

Variegated Meadowhawk
p. 149

Pacific Tiger Beetle
p. 149

**INVERTEBRATES**

Convergent Ladybug
p. 150

Yellow Jackets
p. 150

Bumble Bees
p. 150

Carpenter Ants
p. 151

Giant Crane Flies
p. 151

Green Lacewings
p. 151

Stream Skater
p. 152

Water Boatman
p. 152

Garden Centipedes
p. 152

Clown Millipede
p. 153

Western Black Widow
p. 153

Yellow-orange Banana Slug
p. 153

**TREES**

White Fir
p. 157

Grand Fir
p. 157

Douglas-fir
p. 158

Englemann Spruce
p. 158

Sitka Spruce
p. 159

Western Larch
p. 159

Western Hemlock
p. 160

Western White Pine
p. 160

Shore Pine
p. 161

Ponderosa Pine
p. 161

Western Yew
p. 162

Western Redcedar
p. 162

Garry Oak
p. 163

Red Alder
p. 163

White Birch
p. 164

Black Cottonwood
p. 164

Quaking Aspen
p. 165

Bitter Cherry
p. 165

Pacific Madrone
p. 166

Pacific Dogwood
p. 166

Bigleaf Maple
p. 167

Oregon Ash
p. 167

Common Juniper
p. 169

Prince's-pine
p. 169

Falsebox
p. 169

Common Bearberry
p. 170

**SHRUBS**

Salal
p. 170

Black Huckleberry
p. 170

Grouseberry
p. 171

False Azalea
p. 171

Pacific Rhododendron
p. 171

Pink Mountain-heather
p. 172

Tall Oregon-grape
p. 172

Scouler's Willow
p. 172

Red-osier Dogwood
p. 173

Saskatoon
p. 173

Western Mountain-ash
p. 173

Thimbleberry
p. 174

Ninebark
p. 174

Birch-leaved Spiraea
p. 174

Oceanspray
p. 175

Shrubby Cinquefoil
p. 175

Bitterbrush
p. 175

Scotch Broom
p. 176

Big Sagebrush
p. 176

Rabbitbush
p. 176

Deerbrush
p. 177

Cascara Buckthorn
p. 177

Squaw Currant
p. 177

Bristly Black Currant
p. 178

Common Snowberry
p. 178

Twinberry
p. 178

Black Elderberry
p. 179

Poison Oak
p. 179

Nodding Onion
p. 182

Corn Lily
p. 182

Chocolate Lily
p. 182

False Lily-of-the-Valley
p. 183

Star-flowered False Solomon's-seal
p. 183

Wake Robin
p. 183

Green False-Hellebore
p. 184

Meadow Death Camas
p. 184

Skunk Cabbage
p. 184

Lanceleaf Springbeauty
p. 185

Miner's Lettuce
p. 185

Threeleaf Lewisia
p. 185

Field Chickweed
p. 186

Seabluff Catchfly
p. 186

American Winter Cress
p. 186

Field Mustard
p. 187

Shepherd's Purse
p. 187

Peppergrass
p. 187

California Poppy
p. 188

**HERBS, FERNS & SEAWEEDS**

Pacific Bleeding Heart
p. 188

Brook Saxifrage
p. 188

Small-flowered Woodland Star
p. 189

Foamflower
p. 189

Pacific Sedum
p. 189

Windflower
p. 190

Western Columbine
p. 190

Marsh Marigold
p. 190

Western Buttercup
p. 191

Meadowrue
p. 191

Beach Strawberry
p. 191

Redwood Sorrel
p. 192

Wood Violet
p. 192

Broadleaf Lupine
p. 192

Clovers
p. 193

Winter Vetch
p. 193

Fireweed
p. 193

Cow Parsnip
p. 194

Northern Gentian
p. 194

Western Waterleaf
p. 194

Baby Blue-eyes
p. 195

Varileaf Phacelia
p. 195

Spreading Phlox
p. 195

Pennyroyal
p. 196

Bedstraw
p. 196

Scarlet Paintbrush
p. 196

Yellow Monkeyflower
p. 197

Davidson's Penstemon
p. 197

American Brooklime
p. 197

Twinflower
p. 198

Common Yarrow
p. 198

Leafy Aster
p. 198

Brass Buttons
p. 199

Subalpine Fleabane
p. 199

Common Tarweed
p. 199

Woolly Mule Ears
p. 200

Heart-leaved Arnica
p. 200

Sitka Valerian
p. 200

Bracken Fern
p. 201

Sword Fern
p. 201

Maidenhair Fern
p. 201

Surf Grass
p. 202

Turkish Towel · Red Algae
p. 202

Giant Kelp · Brown Algae
p. 202

Bull Kelp · Brown Algae
p. 203

Sea Lettuce · Green Algae
p. 203

23

The natural regions of Washington and Oregon are well appreciated by both the residents and visitors to these two states. The Pacific Northwest is an area with abundant biodiversity found along the lengths of undeveloped coastline, within its famed temperate rainforest, throughout its various mighty mountain ranges and among the grasslands and sagebrush of the arid interior. Foresight in establishing protected areas and state and national parks has conserved areas of wilderness for us to appreciate and experience today and into the future. Beyond protected borders, parts of Washington and Oregon are still wild enough for foxes, bears and hawks, and remote enough for rare and elusive species such as bobcats and wolves. Our own backyards host visits from bold and opportunistic species such as coyotes, deer and many birds, insects and rodents. We are able to catch sight of whales passing close to our shores, celebrate the great spectacles of migratory birds along our Pacific Flyway in spring and fall, wrap our arms around ancient trees in our great forests and listen to the chorus of frogs that sing about our significant wetlands, lakes and rivers. Some of the most exciting and spectacular wilderness experiences in North America are granted to those of us fortunate enough to live in or visit Washington and Oregon.

Every ecoregion around the world comprises a number of complex habitats; in our area, these habitats include grasslands, agricultural and urban areas, arid sagebush and chaparral scrublands, pine-juniper, deciduous, coniferous and mixed woodlands, riparian and marine zones, fresh- and saltwater wetlands, subalpine tundra and alpine rock and ice. The many unique complexities within the systems of plants and animals are governed by an infrastructure of water, soil, topography, climate and elevation, but we can identify the following ecoregions to highlight the basic biogeography of the two states.

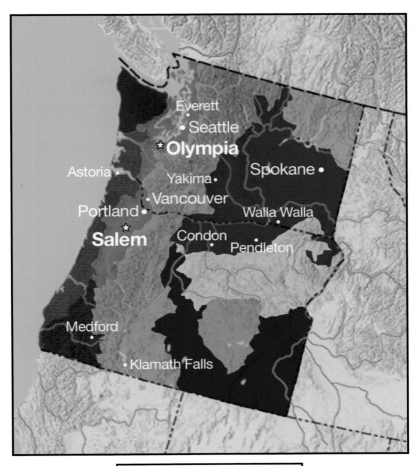

## ECO-REGION LEGEND

- ■ Pacific Coast & Coast Mountains
- ■ Olympic Peninsula
- ■ Klamath Mountains
- ■ Puget Trough & Willamette Valley
- ■ Cascade Mountains
- ■ NE Washington & Selkirk Mountains
- ■ Columbia River Plateau & Basin
- ■ Blue Mountains
- ■ Northern Basin & Range
- ■ Harvey Basin

# THE REGIONS

## Pacific Coast & Coast Mountain Range

The rocky Pacific coastline, with sandy beaches and nutrient-rich estuaries, is bordered by ocean on one side and high coastal mountains covered in lush, temperate forests on the other. The resulting landscape is dramatic in its beauty and its wildlife assemblage. Numerous small cities occur along the coast, and a good balance exists between those cities and the surrounding wilderness. In this ecoregion, you can find gray whales, migrating humpback whales, black bears, mountain lions and Roosevelt elk. The San Juan Islands off Washington's northern shores are famous for their mild climate and low precipitation caused by being in the rain shadow of the Olympic Mountains.

## Olympic Peninsula

This lush region receives the highest annual rainfall of any of the lower 48 states. The result is a moist, temperate rainforest of coniferous trees: mainly Douglas-fir, western hemlock, Sitka spruce and western red cedar. The scenic, snowcapped Olympic Mountains rise above the forest over much of the peninsula, and some of this mountainous area, such as Olympic National Park, is protected. The peninsula is home to a large variety of mammals, including the endemic and endangered Olympic marmot. The open coastline is an excellent place to see sea otters and migrating gray whales.

## Klamath Mountains

Covering much of southwestern Oregon, this ecoregion includes the Umpqua Valley and Siskiyou Mountains as well as the Klamath interior valley cradled between the Klamath and Cascade ranges. The Klamath Mountains have a mosaic of soil types, leading to a high biodiversity of plant life. Within North America, this ecoregion is recognized as one of seven Areas of Global Botanical Significance by the World Conservation Union, with more kinds of cone-bearing trees than anywhere else. From an international perspective, the World Conservation Union notes this ecoregion as a world Center of Plant Diversity, and the World Wildlife Fund deems it an important location worldwide for species diversity. Off the ground, you may see one of several bat species at night or butterfly species by day; in the many rivers and ponds are cutthroat trout and pond turtles.

# Puget Trough & Willamette Valley

The sheltered waters of Puget Sound are a unique biogeographical feature of Washington. Puget Sound alone has more than 1000 miles of coastline and boasts a wealth of marine life and lush, coastal forests with an endemic form of Douglas-fir. Many species of marine mammals can be found here, such as seals, sea-lions and orcas. Geologically and physiographically, the lowlands of the Puget Trough continue as far south as the Willamette Valley in Oregon. This valley has been extensively converted to agriculture, but some of the native oak savannahs, grasslands and wetlands remain. The western fence lizard, western skink, rubber boa, beaver, mule deer, mink, northern river otter, coyote, red fox and even the occasional black bear are seen in these lowlands.

# Cascade Mountains

The high mountains of the Cascade Range were formed from volcanic processes and pass through both Washington and Oregon parallel to the coastline. Although they now sleep under snow and ice, these dormant volcanoes had a dramatic effect on the geological and ecological makeup of the region. Most of the distinctly conical peaks are between 7000 feet and 9000 feet in elevation; the highest is Mount Rainier, in Washington, at 14,410 feet. Wander in the forests of ponderosa pine, interior Douglas-fir, grand fir, oak (on the eastern slopes) and mountain hemlock, and watch for mountain lions, black bears, bobcats, wolverines, deer and endemic Cascade golden-mantled ground squirrels.

# Northeastern Washington & Selkirk Mountains

The high, densely forested northeastern interior of Washington lacks the moderating influence of the ocean, and its winters are colder than elsewhere in the state. Animals from farther north, which are adapted to cold climates, can be found here. In the northeastern corner of the state are the Selkirk Mountains, actually part of the much more extensive Rocky Mountains. Here you might encounter the elusive caribou, whose population, numbering only about 100, is considered endangered. In addition to caribou, the Selkirks have the only stable population of grizzly bears and moose in either Washington or Oregon. Grizzly bears are also reported in the northern Cascades, but their numbers are probably very small.

# Columbia River Plateau & Columbia Basin

Boxed in by the Cascade, Okanogan, Rocky and Blue mountains, the Columbia Plateau is a flood basalt plateau that lies across parts of both Washington and Oregon. It is diverse, with sage and bitterbrush scrubland interspersed with grassland steppes. The semi-arid agricultural heartland is irrigated by the Columbia and Snake rivers, and the animals and plants that live on the Columbia Plateau are well adapted to dry conditions, summer heat and winter cold. Look for pronghorns in the grasslands and sandhill cranes in the wetlands and agricultural areas.

The Columbia Plateau overlaps a portion of the Columbia Basin in eastern Washington and north-central Oregon. The Columbia Basin is the drainage basin of the Columbia River, which pours from the Rocky Mountains into the Pacific Ocean. The Columbia Basin is also warm and dry, an open region strongly affected by the rain shadow effect of both the Olympic and Cascade mountains. Geologically, this basin was formed by the action of glaciers during the ice age, though the Columbia River and some major flooding events have reshaped much of the landscape since then. Shrubby vegetation and numerous small lakes and marshes characterize this region. Many mammals are found throughout the basin region, including bobcats, coyotes, badgers and yellow-bellied marmots. The Columbia Basin tilts southward into the Great Basin, which extends into a small portion of eastern Oregon.

# Northern Basin & Range

The Northern Basin and Range ecoregion in southeastern Oregon is the northern fringe of the Great Basin, which covers the large, arid region of the western United States and has no natural outlet to the sea. In Oregon, it is a salt sagebrush country of dry ancient lakes, sand dunes and white alkali playas with tall fault ridges jutting up from the flat earth. Being in the rain shadow of the Cascades makes this ecoregion Oregon's driest. Sagebrush dominates, but aspen groves and mountain mahogany are common, with rare stands of white fir. A great number of reptiles enjoy the dry heat of this region, and many species typical of the Southwest find their northerly ranges here.

# Harney Basin

The Harney Basin of south-central and southeastern Oregon is bordered to the north by the Blue Mountains and the Columbia Basin. Like the Columbia Basin, it was formed primarily by glacial activity during the most recent ice age. Today, the landscape is exhilarating in its sweeping vistas and long horizons. Although the basin region appears stark by comparison to the lush forests in western Oregon, it boasts a unique environment of arid sagebrush flats interspersed with clear ponds and nutrient-rich marshes. Birds are abundant here, and some of the mammals you might encounter include ground squirrels, black-tailed jackrabbits, mule deer, coyotes, common muskrats and even the majestic bighorn sheep. The rare kit fox—more typical of drier desert regions farther south—reaches its northern limit here.

# Blue Mountains

The Blue Mountains in the southeastern corner of Washington and of northeastern Oregon consist of high basalt ridges, low valleys, arid grasslands, lush marshes and pristine lakes. Much of these mountains are covered in coniferous forests—Engelmann spruce, for example, at high elevations, with Douglas-fir and ponderosa pine lower on the slopes leading down to shrubby high canyons of juniper, sagebrush and bitterbrush. Winters in this region are tougher than in the warmer areas to the west, but they are not as harsh as in the mountains to the north. This range sits between the Rocky and Cascade mountains, and although it has characteristics of both, it is more similar to the Rockies. East of the Blue Mountains are the Wallowa Mountains; this small range is biologically even more similar to the Rocky Mountains than are the Blue Mountains. Watch for charismatic mountain species such as elk, bighorn sheep, mink, northern river otter and beaver.

# HUMAN-ALTERED LANDSCAPES & URBAN ENVIRONMENTS

The impact of human activity on natural environments is visible throughout Washington and Oregon. No brief outline of important habitats would be complete without a mention of the towns and cities of these states. Roads, urban and agricultural areas, and forestry and mining sites are just a few examples of the impact we have had on the landscape. The pattern of settlement is predominantly along the coast, with smaller cities scattered throughout the mountains and beyond into the interior.

Biodiversity is at its highest along the suburban fringe, where a botanical anarchy of remnant native plants, exotic introduced plants and hybrids exist. Strategic species, whether native or introduced, take advantage of evolving opportunities for food, shelter and breeding territory. We have established human-made lakes, urban parks bird feeders, birdhouses and bat houses to deliberately accommodate the species we appreciate, while wharves and ports, garbage dumps and our own homes seem to attract the species we don't appreciate and consider to be pests. Many of the most common plants and animals in these altered landscapes were not present before the arrival of settlers and modern transportation. The most established of the introduced species exemplify how co-habitation with humans offers a distinct set of living situations for many plants and animals. House mice, Norway rats and, most recently, nutrias are some of the highly successful exotic animals that have been introduced to North America from other continents.

# THE SEASONS

The seasons of Washington and Oregon greatly influence the lives of plants and animals. Although some birds, insects and marine mammals are migratory, most animals are confined to relatively slow forms of terrestrial travel. As a result, they have limited geographic ranges and must cope in various ways with the changing seasons.

With rising temperatures, reduced snow or rain and the greening of the landscape, spring brings renewal. Many animals bear their young at this time of year. The abundance of food travels through the food chain: lush new plant growth provides ample food for herbivores, and the numerous herbivore young become easy prey for carnivores. While some small mammals, particularly rodents, mature within weeks, offspring of the large mammals depend on their parents for much longer periods.

During summer, animals have recovered from the strain of the previous winter's food scarcity and spring's reproductive efforts, but it is not a time of relaxation. To prepare yet again for the upcoming fall and winter, some animals must eat vast quantities of food to build up fat reserves, while others work furiously to stockpile food caches in safe places. Some of the more charismatic species, such as the bugling bull elk—which demonstrates extremes of aggression and vigilance— mate in the fall, and some small mammals, such as voles and mice, mate every few months or even year round.

Winter differs in intensity and duration throughout these two states. In coastal and southern areas, west of the Cascades, winters are mild and do not create much stress for animals. To the east and in high ranges of the mountains, and of course in the more northerly ranges, winter can be an arduous, life-threatening challenge for many creatures. For herbivores, high-energy foods are difficult to find, often requiring more energy to locate than they provide in return. This negative energy balance gradually weakens most herbivores through the winter, and they in turn provide food for the equally needy carnivores. Voles and mice also find advantages in the season—an insulating layer of snow protects their elaborate trails from the worst of winter's cold. Food, shelter and warmth are all found in the thin layer between the snow and the ground surface, and the months devoted to food storage now pay off.

The seasons also affect species composition. The array of species differs from west to east and from winter to summer in those regions. When you visit the interior or mountainous regions in winter, for example, you will see a different group of species than in summer: many plants die back, migrating animals head south, and other animals become dormant in winter; conversely, many birds arrive at winter bird feeders, and certain mammals, such as deer, enter lowland meadows to find edible vegetation, making these species more visible in winter.

31

# OBSERVING NATURE

Many animals are most active at night, so the best times for viewing them are during the "wildlife hours" at dawn and at dusk when they are out of their day-time hideouts or roosting sites. During winter, hunger may force some mammals to be more active during midday. Conversely, in warm seasons, some animals may become less active and less visible in the heat of the day. Within the protected reserves and national parks of Washington and Oregon, many larger mammals can be viewed easily from the safety of a vehicle. If you walk back-country trails, however, you are typically in the territory of certain mammals with which encounters are best avoided unless from a distance.

Birdwatching is popular activity among serious "birders" and people who simply wish to recognize and appreciate the diversity of attractive and interesting birds. Guidebooks, online resources and clubs and organizations are all abundant and accessible for those interested in learning more about local birdlife. Birdwatching is both relaxing and a ready source of mental and physical exercise. One must be patient, though, because birds are among the most highly mobile animals; they may be seen one moment and then vanish the next!

Whale watching can be an organized activity, with boats taking groups of tourists out to known areas of high whale and dolphin sightings, or, because many species frequent inshore waters, it can be a random moment of fortune right from the shore. Although whale watching has strong merit for encouraging public awareness and appreciation for marine mammals and the health of the oceans, it can disrupt cetacean behavior, and tour groups must be considerate and passive in the presence of these sensitive species.

Although more people have become conscious of the need to protect wildlife, human pressures have nevertheless damaged critical habitats, and some species experience frequent harassment. Modern wildlife viewing demands courtesy and common sense. Honor both the encounter and the animal by demonstrating a respect appropriate to the occasion. Here are some points to remember for ethical wildlife watching in the field:

• Stress is harmful to wildlife, so never chase or flush animals from cover or try to catch or touch them. Use binoculars and keep a respectful distance, for the animal's sake and often for your own. Amphibians are especially sensitive to being touched or held—sunscreen or insect repellant on your skin can poison the animal.

• Leave the environment, including both flora and fauna, unchanged by your visits. Tread lightly and take home only pictures and memories. Do not pick wildflowers, and do not collect sea stars, sea urchins or seashells still occupied by the sea animal.

• Fishing is a great way to get in touch with nature, and many anglers appreciate the non-consumptive ethos of catch-and-release.

• Pets hinder wildlife viewing. They may chase, injure or kill other animals, so control your pets or leave them at home.

• Take the time to learn about wildlife and the behavior and sensitivity of each species.

# NATIONAL PARKS & WILDLIFE WATCHING AREAS

Below is just a sampling of the parks and natural areas you may wish to explore, but don't forget that even city parks offer ample opportunity to revel in nature and see many species of plants and animals.

## Washington

### Olympic National Park

The world-famous Olympic National Park contains some of the most beautiful and pristine temperate rainforest in the world. Miles and miles of trails offer excellent opportunities to see the indigenous flora and fauna of the region. Throughout the park, look for Olympic marmots, mountain lions, bobcats, black bears, mule deer and squirrels. The park includes a small, isolated portion on the coast, south of Cape Flattery, where you may see albino deer, harbor seals and California sea lions. Cape Flattery itself offers abundant views of marine life and dramatic scenery. Several trails along the coast provide chances to see wildlife, particularly see sea otters, but watch for gray whales and other marine mammals as well.

### Mount Rainier National Park

The impressive vertical ascent of Mount Rainier creates two distinct ecological zones on the east and west slopes. If you climb the western slopes, you will walk through forests of Douglas-fir and western hemlock, housing birds such as ruffed grouse and red-breasted sapsuckers, then through silver fir. Starting up the drier eastern slopes, you walk through oak and then ponderosa pine forests, where you can see various species of woodpeckers. Don't miss the old-growth forests of the Cathedral Grove on the eastern flank of the mountain near the Stevens Canyon entrance on SR 706. Hemlocks and fir cloak the low elevation slopes, transitioning to pine forests. Vegetation becomes more stunted and sparse entering the subalpine zone, and the most obvious wildlife are the corvids such as magpies and crows, and rodents. Only the hardiest of plants are seen once you pass the treeline into the snowy, icy alpine zone. Overall, the scenic beauty of Mount Rainier National Park is one of the great prides of our nation.

## San Juan Island

Remote and beautiful, San Juan Island is the perfect place for viewing marine mammals. Several sites on this island, such as Lime Kiln Point State Park and Cattle Point, offer the best chances of seeing minke whales and killer whales. Other mammals to look for include harbor seals and northern river otters.

## North Cascades National Park

North Cascades National Park offers exceptional opportunities for wildlife viewing amid dramatic mountain scenery. Grizzly bears and gray wolves are infrequently reported here, and your chances of seeing either are low. The most likely mammals to see include Cascade golden-mantled ground squirrels, hoary marmots, other squirrels and chipmunks, coyotes, mule deer, elk and black bears.

## Flume Creek Mountain Goat Viewing Area

Perhaps the best place in Washington for viewing hoofed mammals, Flume Creek provides outstanding chances to see wildlife found nowhere else in Washington. The forests, high-elevation grassy plateaus and wetlands are prime habitat for moose, white-tailed deer and mule deer. Mountain goats are frequently seen in the rockier areas, as are bighorn sheep. Flume Creek also has the only resident population of caribou in the state. Look for these elegant northern animals in high meadows.

## Palouse Falls State Park

Palouse Falls may not offer the best chances for seeing large carnivores and hoofed mammals, but the sheer dramatic beauty of the waterfall makes up for it. The spectacular basin and waterfall were formed during violent flooding events about 12,000 years ago. Look for yellow-bellied marmots, mountain cottontails, white-tailed jackrabbits and the occasional white-tailed deer.

## Mount Spokane State Park

Mount Spokane State Park provides wildlife watching opportunities close to a major urban area. Conifers such as Douglas-fir, ponderosa pine, spruce and hemlock provide habitat for many species at any time of year, but particularly in winter and spring when shelter and breeding and nesting sites are important. During migration periods, high elevations can be good for raptors. High, open, grassy and rocky areas may turn up horned larks, spring meadows will display lupines and paintbrushes, and the river is full of trout.

# WASHINGTON & OREGON NATIONAL PARKS AND WILDLIFE VIEWING AREAS

# NATIONAL PARKS & WILDLIFE WATCHING AREAS

## WASHINGTON

1. Olympic National Park
2. San Juan Island
3. Samish and Skagit Flats
4. Fort Casey State Park
5. Ocean Shores and Grays Harbor
6. North Cascades National Park
7. Sinlahekin Wildlife Area
8. Conconully State Park
9. Mountain Loop Highway
10. Mount Rainier National Park
11. Lone Butte Wildlife Emphasis Area
12. Ridgefield National Wildlife Refuge Complex
13. Quilomene Wildlife Area
14. Flume Creek Mountain Goat Viewing Area
15. Mount Spokane State Park
16. Turnbull National Wildlife Refuge
17. Palouse Falls State Park
18. McNary National Wildlife Refuge

## OREGON

19. Fort Stevens State Park
20. Highway 101
21. Oaks Bottom Wildlife Refuge
22. Ankeny National Wildlife Refuge
23. Rimrock Springs Wildlife Management Area
24. Tumalo State Park
25. Deschutes National Forest
26. Denman Wildlife Area
27. Klamath Marsh National Wildlife Refuge
28. Wallowa Lake State Park
29. Elkhorn Wildlife Area
30. Malheur National Wildlife Refuge
31. Hart Mountain National Antelope Refuge

## Fort Casey State Park

The woods of Fort Casey State Park are excellent for a wide variety of birds. Adjacent to the park is Keystone Harbor on Crocket Lake and Whidbey Island. Whidbey Island provides many different habitats. Sea-level Crockett Lake, with its open water and mudflats, is separated from Admiralty Inlet by a grassy and sandy spit. Adjoining both is Keystone Harbor. The entire area is excellent spot for seeing shorebirds during the southbound migration period from early July to late September. From the Washington State Ferry from Keystone Harbor to Port Townsend, you can see cormorants, loons, grebes and gulls. The birds are attracted to the abundant fish that thrive in the cold, nutrient-rich waters of Admiralty Inlet. You can walk onto the ferry, or you can drive aboard. Dress warmly (even in summer) and hang out on the upper deck for the best view.

## Turnbull National Wildlife Refuge

Turnbull National Wildlife Refuge is an oasis in dry eastern Washington. Much of the refuge is off-limits to the public, but a loop road takes you through open ponderosa pine forest and alongside ponds and lakes, where many species of breeding waterfowl can be seen in spring. The pine forest and riparian vegetation is good for woodpeckers, chickadees, nuthatches, sapsuckers, flycatchers, vireos, wrens and many other birds, with unusual species turning up during migration periods (April to May and August to October). While you quietly birdwatch, you may see whitetailed deer, long-tailed weasels, red squirrels, coyotes and northern river otters.

## Lone Butte Wildlife Emphasis Area

The meadows and mixed forests of Lone Butte are good places for peaceful wildlife viewing. Several trails expose visitors to the riparian forests and mixed coniferous forests that characterize much of the area. The luckiest visitors here may see black bears, northern river otters, coyotes, red foxes, mule deer and beavers.

## Samish and Skagit Flats

Fall and winter birding is outstanding on the open fields of the Samish and Skagit flats, with opportunities to see raptors, shorebirds and waterfowl. At Skagit Flats, watch the open fields, poles and fencelines for raptors. The Skagit Wildlife Area features riparian woodlands along the Skagit River as well as sloughs in open fields. Walking the dikes out to Skagit Bay brings you into an area of marsh and open water great for observing all sorts of wildlife.

## Ridgefield National Wildlife Refuge Complex

Ridgefield has numerous ponds and marshes throughout the thousands of acres of wetlands, grasslands and woodlands. The wetlands are important wintering and migratory staging grounds for huge populations of ducks and geese and a small population of sandhill cranes; the shrubby and grassy areas are good for spotting sparrows, rabbits and coyotes; and the oak woodlands are home to forest birds such as woodpeckers and owls, as well as squirrels and deer. The complex comprises the Ridgefield, Steigerwald Lake, Franz Lake and Pierce national wildlife refuges.

## McNary National Wildlife Refuge

On the shore of Lake Wallula is McNary National Wildlife Refuge, where the marshes, fields and open water provide excellent habitat for birds, especially waterfowl. Incredible concentrations of Canada geese and mallards thrive here alongside other species, including green-winged teals, ring-necked ducks and lesser scaups. There are thousands of colonial nesting shorebirds and significant numbers of rarer species such as bald eagles and peregrine falcons. The wetlands and shoreline bays also provide habitat for amphibians, invertebrates and aquatic mammals and serve as an important nursery for developing fall Chinook salmon.

## Ocean Shores and Grays Harbor

Ocean Shores, in Grays Harbor County, is on a long peninsula that separates Grays Harbor from the Pacific Ocean on the outer coast. Every season offers a new wildlife watching opportunity. Check out the Point Brown jetty to see winter shorebirds, loons, grebes, cormorants, sea ducks, gulls, terns and brown pelicans. Winter storms may bring rarely seen pelagic birds close to shore. In spring or fall, you may wish to explore Oyhut Wildlife Recreation Area, adjacent to the jetty area. On the Grays Harbor side of the peninsula is Damon Point State Park, where shorebirds forage at low tide and interesting insect and plant life can be seen on the grass-covered dunes—also the site of a nesting area for snowy plovers, so please observe the closure signs during the spring breeding season. Ocean City State Park has freshwater ponds with fish and frogs. Forests twitter with warblers and squirrels. Huge gatherings of shorebirds occur in April in Grays Harbor National Wildlife Refuge and Bowerman Basin, including approximately 90% of the western sandpiper population. Another great location to observe migrating shorebirds is at Bottle Beach State Park on the south shore of Grays Harbor.

## Sinlahekin Wildlife Area

The Sinlahekin Wildlife Area, in the Sinlahekin Valley, is the oldest wildlife area in the state. On the far northeastern flank of the Okanogan Mountains, spring and summer feature some of the highest breeding bird diversity in Washington. Palmer Lake and Champneys Slough, among other wetlands in the valley, host abundant birdlife and aquatic species of plants and animals.

## Mountain Loop Highway

If you prefer wildlife encounters from the safety of your vehicle, driving the Mountain Loop Highway is an excellent way to see the local wildlife. The trip lasts about three hours and takes you through riparian zones, mountain forests and alpine habitat. Watch for mule deer, coyotes, squirrels and mountain goats. From the trails along this route, you may see beavers, northern river otters and red foxes.

## Conconully State Park

This park offers some of the best boreal birding in Washington. In the transition from ponderosa pine into a zone with larch, you can spot various species of woodpeckers and flycatchers. Conconully Lake and Roger Lake are good birdwatching areas. Driving the forest roads (in summer only) takes you to higher elevations and forest habitats.

## Quilomene Wildlife Area

Quilomene Wildlife Area, near the town of Vantage, protects some relatively pristine sage–shrub steppe habitat where sparrows, hares, snakes and the buzz of insects will catch your attention in spring and summer. The Columbia River passes along this area, and the rocky cliffs along the coulee are home to cliff-dwelling swallows. Various other animals frequent the shores for a drink. Ginkgo Petrified Forest State Park offers good views over the Columbia River, and you can also visit the park's museum. In winter and spring, check out Wanapum State Park. Wanapum Lake, formed by the Wanapum Dam downstream from Vantage, is excellent in winter for seeing loons and grebes and in spring for many atypical bird species migrating through the area.

# Oregon

## Malheur National Wildlife Refuge

Malheur is best known for its migrant geese and ducks, but an equally impressive attraction is the great number of sandhill cranes that stage here. Other regular species include American white pelicans and burrowing owls. During spring and fall migration, songbirds find appropriate habitat around the refuge headquarters, and hummingbirds can be seen hovering among the colorful flowers. Nesting marsh birds, shorebirds and gulls spend summer here and are seen most abundantly at the Narrows area between Malheur Lake and Mud Lake. Woodpeckers, squirrels and other forest dwellers can be seen up in the heights of the lodgepole pines in Malheur National Forest.

## Klamath Marsh National Wildlife Refuge

This wildlife refuge encompasses extensive wetlands, meadows and forests. A wide variety of birds, amphibians and mammals dwell in such a diverse habitat. Miller Island is a migration resting area for large numbers of Canada geese and tundra swans from late February to late April. Along with dozens of bird species in the refuge, look for yellow-pine chipmunks, mountain cottontails, northern river otters, raccoons, mule deer and Rocky Mountain elk. The large lake north of Klamath Falls has various species of grebe, as well as cormorants and pelicans, all nesting together. Upper Klamath National Wildlife Refuge's wet marshland is best explored by canoe, and the Lower Klamath National Wildlife Refuge offers self-guided auto tours.

## Highway 101

All along the Oregon portion of Highway 101 are world-class state parks and wildlife refuges where you can see the abundant coastal flora and fauna of Oregon. The highway parallels the coast, as do migrating gray whales and humpback whales. In March, April and May, watch for whales from the headlands. Few other spots in the world offer such outstanding opportunities to see marine mammals from land. The tide pool life along this route is exceptional, but remember that most state parks prohibit collecting and touching tide pool life, and in some places, trespassing is also prohibited. On coastal rocks and rocky islets, look for sea-lions and harbor seals. Along the length of the highway and its numerous walking trails, watch for mule deer, Roosevelt elk, black bears, raccoons, northern river otters, brush rabbits and mountain beavers. In the south of Oregon along this route at night, you might even see a ringtail.

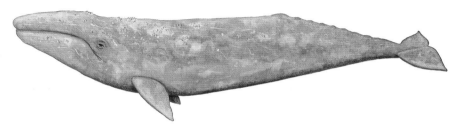

## Denman Wildlife Area

The excellent wetlands and lush forests of the Denman Wildlife Area provide homes for a wide variety of birds, reptiles and amphibians. The mammals are also diverse here, but most mammals tend to be more secretive than birds. Along the trails and open areas of this park, look for beavers, common muskrats, northern river otters, western gray squirrels, black-tailed jackrabbits and deer.

## Ankeny National Wildlife Refuge

Founded in 1960, Ankeny was set aside as one of three preserves in Oregon for the dusky race of Canada goose. Boardwalks provide great viewing opportunities with little disturbance of nesting birds, including goldfinches. Trails near numerous ponds allow you to see the grebes, geese and ducks that gather on the water in large numbers during the day and the dunlins that typically gather in late afternoon in enormous flocks to roost. Watch for geese and raptors in winter.

### Hart Mountain National Antelope Refuge

As its name suggests, this wildlife refuge was developed to protect the habitat of the pronghorn and ensure a stable population. Of course, other animals that live in the same habitat enjoy the protection that this refuge offers. This area encompasses wetlands, sagebrush flats, grasslands, rugged canyons and aspen groves. In addition to pronghorns, look for ground squirrels, black-tailed jackrabbits, coyotes, mule deer and bighorn sheep along the trails and roads of this refuge.

### Rimrock Springs Wildlife Management Area

A wide variety of plants and animals make their home in the protected habitats of the Rimrock Springs Wildlife Management Area. This area includes marshlands, grasslands, sagebrush flats and riparian zones. Birds and mammals are abundant and diverse here, and visitors frequently see yellow-pine chipmunks, mountain cottontails, porcupines, beavers, coyotes, mule deer and pronghorns.

### Wallowa Lake State Park

Wallowa Lake State Park is in the scenic Blue Mountains of northeastern Oregon and encompasses beautiful mountain lakes and thick forests. Watch for golden-mantled ground squirrels, raccoons, striped skunks, porcupines, mink, Rocky Mountain elk and mule deer. The Upper Wallowa Valley is one of eastern Oregon's best birding areas year round. The Wallowa Fish Hatchery is also good for wildlife watching.

### Tumalo State Park

In Tumalo State Park, you can hike the trails alongside the Deschutes River, fish the trout streams or canoe and swim in the alpine lakes. Swifts and swallows can be seen along the cliffs of the river's canyon walls; coyotes can be heard yipping and howling at night. The Cascade Mountains add to the scenery, and sage and juniper scent the air.

### Elkhorn Wildlife Area

Some of the best opportunities to see Rocky Mountain elk in Oregon can be found in the Elkhorn Wildlife Area. In fall, you may even hear the haunting calls of a bugling bull elk. This area was protected to serve as a feeding range for elk during winter. Because agricultural land has taken over so much of the native grasslands, elk used to rely on agricultural forage to survive winter.

### Fort Stevens State Park

The largest campground in Oregon is at Fort Stevens State Park, where you can camp year round at Coffenbury Lake, find rewarding birdwatching opportunities, fish from the Columbia River, where over one million salmon and steelhead run, and enjoy miles of beautiful ocean beach. An early-morning walk around the trail that winds around the lake offers the best chance to see breeding birds and migrants. Nesting waterbirds include wood ducks and mergansers, and gulls, terns and wrentits can be seen all year. Loons and grebes can be seen from the jetty in fall, and the Jetty Lagoon is a good place to look for bald eagles and peregrine falcons. Historical attractions include the wreck of the *Peter Iredale* and Fort Stevens, the only military installation in the continental United States to have been fired on since the War of 1812.

### Deschutes National Forest

Along the eastern slopes of the Cascade Mountains of central Oregon, Deschutes National Forest comprises over 1.6 million acres of dense alpine coniferous forests and alpine meadows. Jays and warblers can be seen in the forest, and plenty of woodpeckers can be heard if not seen. Nearby is the Newberry National Volcanic Monument.

### Oaks Bottom Wildlife Refuge

Oaks Bottom Wildlife Refuge in southeastern Portland is home to great blue herons and wood ducks in the wetter areas, and the woodlots contain plenty of migrant songbirds. Portland offers other "urban" wildlife-watching opportunities. Crystal Springs Rhododendron Garden has warblers and waterfowl that you can watch at close range. The Audubon Society of Portland's Pittock Bird Sanctuary has an excellent visitor's center, and the sanctuary is surrounded by dense coniferous forest in a steep ravine. Forest Park in northwest Portland is one of the largest city parks in the United States and is best known for its spring and early-summer nighttime owling.

# ANIMALS

Animals are mammals, birds, reptiles, amphibians, fish and invertebrates, all of which belong to the Kingdom Animalia. They obtain energy by ingesting food that they hunt or gather. Mammals and birds are endothermic, meaning that body temperature is internally regulated and will stay nearly constant despite the surrounding environmental temperature unless that temperature is extreme and persistent. Reptiles, amphibians, fish and invertebrates are ectothermic, meaning that they do not have the ability to generate their own internal body temperature and tend to be the same temperature as their surroundings. Animals reproduce sexually, and they have a limited growth that is reached at sexual maturity. They also have diverse and complicated behaviours displayed in courtship, defense, parenting, playing, fighting, eating, hunting, in their social hierarchy, and in how they deal with environmental stresses such as weather, change of season or availability of food and water.

# MAMMALS

**M**ammals are the group to which human beings belong. The general characteristics of a mammal include being endothermic, bearing live young (with the exception of the platypus and echidnas), nursing their young and having hair or fur on their bodies. In general, all mammals larger than rodents are sexually dimorphic, meaning that the male and the female are different in appearance by size or other diagnostics such as antlers. Males are usually larger than females. Different groups of mammals include herbivores, carnivores, omnivores or insectivores. People often associate large mammals with wilderness, making these animals prominent symbols in native legends and stirring emotional connections with people in modern times.

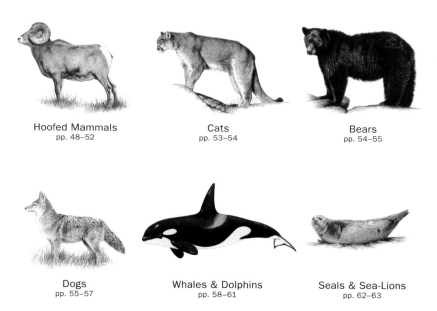

Hoofed Mammals
pp. 48–52

Cats
pp. 53–54

Bears
pp. 54–55

Dogs
pp. 55–57

Whales & Dolphins
pp. 58–61

Seals & Sea-Lions
pp. 62–63

**Otters**
pp. 63–64

**Weasels & Skunks**
pp. 64–67

**Raccoons**
p. 67

**Porcupine**
p. 68

**Beavers & Nutria**
pp. 68–69

**Mice & Kin**
pp. 69–72

**Squirrels**
pp. 72–74

**Hares & Rabbits**
pp. 74–76

**Pika**
p. 76

**Bats**
pp. 76–78

**Moles & Shrews**
pp. 78–79

**Opossum**
p. 79

# Mountain Goat

### *Oreamnos americanus*

**Length:** 4–5 ft (tail 3½–5½ in)
**Shoulder height:** 3–4 ft
**Weight:** 100–300 lb

Watching a mountain goat climbing or descending the steep rocky slopes of their high alpine home can leave observers feeling on edge, but this animal is more than comfortable on precarious cliffs and high precipices. A mountain goat's anatomy is such that it can place and maneuver all 4 hooves on a ledge as small as 6 × 2 in. • Within hours of being born, playful mountain goat kids are able to run, jump and climb. **Where found:** steep slopes and rocky cliffs in alpine or subalpine areas throughout the Coast, Cascade and Olympic mountains.

# Bighorn Sheep

### *Ovis canadensis*

**Length:** 5–6 ft (tail 3–5 in)
**Shoulder height:** 30–45 in
**Weight:** 120–340 lb

Male bighorn sheep have spectacular horns and engage them in head-butting clashes during fall rut. Both sexes have brown horns, but the females' are short and do not curve around with the impressiveness of the males'. • Once extirpated from Washington, the bighorn subspecies from California, *O. c. californiana*, was successfully reintroduced. Mountain meadows provide feeding grounds, and rocky outcroppings provide protection from predators, namely eagles, mountain lions and bobcats, which prey on the lambs. **Where found:** rugged mountain slopes, cliffs and alpine meadows; range extends from California north to the Rocky Mountains of Canada. **Also known as:** mountain sheep.

# Pronghorn

### *Antilocapra americana*

**Length:** 4–5 ft (tail 3½–6 in)
**Shoulder height:** 32–41 in
**Weight:** 70–140 lb

Often incorrectly referred to as an antelope, the pronghorn is actually the sole member of the family Antilocapridae (true antelopes belong to the Bovidae family along with cows, goats and sheep). Its branched horns are shed like antlers. • The pronghorn is the fastest animal in the Western Hemisphere, able to retain continuous 20-ft bounds at up to 60 mph, yet it cannot jump a fence. Fences in managed pronghorn territory are higher for the animal to duck underneath, which it can do at a full run without breaking stride. **Where found:** the grasslands of southwestern Oregon.

# Elk

### *Cervus elaphus*

**Length:** 6–9 ft (tail 4½–7 in)
**Shoulder height:** 4–5 ft
**Weight:** 400–1000 lb

The haunting, high-pitched bugle calls of rutting male elk are a hallmark of fall. A male's large, spreading antlers may span 5 ft and weigh up to 30 lb. During fall rut and in spring when females are with calves, elk can be very dangerous and should be avoided. • There are 2 subspecies of elk in Washington and Oregon: Rocky Mountain elk (*C. e. nelsoni*) on the eastern slopes of the Cascades and Roosevelt elk (*C. e. roosevelti*) on the western slopes. **Where found:** upland forests and grasslands, ranging into coniferous forests and alpine tundra; higher elevations in spring and lower elevations in fall. **Also known as:** wapiti.

# Mule Deer

### *Odocoileus hemionus*

**Length:** 4–6 ft (tail 4½–9 in)
**Shoulder height:** 3–3½ ft
**Weight:** 68–470 lb

Mule deer form large bands, particularly in winter. They escape predators with bounding hops called "stotting" or "pronking." Large, mule-like ears and a black-tipped tail are the best field marks for this ungulate. • Two subspecies of mule deer occur in our area: the Columbian deer (*O. h. columbianus*) in coastal regions and the Rocky Mountain mule deer (*O. h. hemionus*) east of the Cascades. **Where found:** hilly terrain, from dry brushlands to high tundra; near streams in dry regions. Bucks tend to remain at higher elevations while does and fawns remain at lower elevations. **Also known as:** black-tailed deer.

# White-tailed Deer

### *Odocoileus virginianus*

**Length:** 4½–7 ft (tail 8–14 in)
**Shoulder height:** 27–45 in
**Weight:** 110–440 lb

A wagging white tail disappearing into the forest is a typical view of this pretty deer. When a mother deer is feeding, she will leave her scentless, spotted fawn behind among tall grasses or shrubs to hide it from potential predators. • A dense network of blood vessels coated by hair, called velvet, covers the developing antlers of males in spring and summer. **Where found:** rolling country with open areas near cover; valleys and stream courses, woodlands, meadows and abandoned farmsteads with tangled shelterbelts; from Canada south, reaching the southernmost extent of its range at the California border. **Also known as:** Virginia deer.

# Moose

### *Alces alces*

**Length:** 8–10 ft (tail 3½–7½ in)
**Shoulder height:** 5½–7 ft
**Weight:** 500–1180 lb

Moose have been known to dive to depths of over 13 ft to find aquatic plants rich in salts and minerals—and to escape those nasty, biting insects! They browse on trees and shrubs and graze on grasses and forbs.
• Moose are the largest deer in the world. Long legs and high steps make the moose well adapted for walking through bogs and deep snow without expending excess energy. **Where found:** in and around lakes, bogs and riparian valleys; coniferous forests and willow and poplar groves; northeastern Washington, with the most stable population in the Selkirks.

# Caribou

### *Rangifer tarandus*

**Length:** 5½–8 ft (tail 5–9 in)
**Shoulder height:** 3–5½ ft
**Weight:** 200–240 lb

Woodland caribou are the only members of the deer family in North America with antlers on both sexes: the female's are slender and the male's are large and C-shaped. Large, crescent-shaped hooves, a long throat mane and well-furred ears and muzzle make caribou superbly adapted for surviving harsh winters. • Caribou migrate to different elevations between seasons. In winter, tree lichens form the bulk of their diet. **Where found:** old-growth coniferous forests of spruce, fir, pine and aspen, moving to the subalpine and alpine meadows in summer; the Selkirk Mountains.

51

# Feral Horse

### *Equus caballus*

**Length:** up to 7 ft (tail up to 3 ft)
**Shoulder height:** 3½–5½ ft
**Weight:** 590–860 lb

Although the domesticated horse is common throughout North America, the existence of the wild horse sparks the romantic imagination of many people who see this introduced species as a symbol of freedom and a vestige of what remains wild in the West. Feral horses are descendant of domestic horses but have run wild for hundreds of years, from the Rocky Mountains to the Southwest. • Wild horses are distinguishable from domestic horses by their long manes and tails and by their pronounced behavioral patterns between members of the herd. **Where found:** small populations occur in the southeast of our region. **Also known as:** mustang.

# Feral Pig

### *Sus scrofa*

**Length:** 4½–6 ft (tail up to 12 in)
**Shoulder height:** 21–43 in
**Weight:** *Male:* 165–440 lb; *Female:* 77–330 lb

One typically thinks of a chubby, pink, bald, docile animal when envisioning a pig. Pigs were bred to lose many of their wild features, which include a coarse, dense fur coat, long, straight, sparsely furred tails and tusks (or modified canines). However, that domestic pig is the same species as its wild relative introduced to North America from Europe and Asia. The wild pig is not docile in its demeanor, either, but dangerously aggressive. It now exists in isolated populations. **Where found:** forested mountain and brushy areas, marshes and ravines or ridges. **Also known as:** wild boar, wild pig, wild hog.

# Mountain Lion

### *Felis concolor*

**Length:** 6–9 ft (tail 25–38 in)
**Shoulder height:** 26–32 in
**Weight:** 70–190 lb

This secretive cat is seldom seen by people, but the occasionally found track or scratch mark indicates that parts of Washington and Oregon are still wild enough for the powerful and majestic mountain lion.

• A mountain lion will sit in a tree above an animal trail, waiting to pounce upon its prey—mainly deer—but other prey opportunities such as other ungulates, beavers, rabbits or birds will not be passed up. **Where found:** montane regions; may occur in brushlands or subalpine regions based on food availability; throughout Washington and Oregon, except the Columbia Basin, though in very low densities. **Also known as:** cougar, puma.

# Canada Lynx

### *Lynx canadensis*

**Length:** 31–40 in (tail 3½–5 in)
**Shoulder height:** 18–23 in
**Weight:** 15–40 lb

With long legs and huge, snowshoe-like paws, the lynx is uniquely adapted for catching snowshoe hares on snow. Lynx and hare populations, accompanied by the hare's food availability, are directly influential; cyclical increases and decreases in hare populations cause lynx populations to follow similar trends. • The facial ruff, long, black ear tufts and black-tipped, short tail are distinctive features. The coat is gray to orange-brown. **Where found:** dense, old-growth coniferous forests with heavy undergrowth; the Selkirk Mountains and the northern Cascades.

# Bobcat

### *Lynx rufus*

**Length:** 2½–4 ft (tail 5–7 in)
**Shoulder height:** 17–20 in
**Weight:** 15–29 lb

The nocturnal bobcat feeds on a wide range of prey including rabbits, voles, mice, birds, reptiles and insects. Small but mighty, the bobcat is even capable of bringing down a deer by the throat if the opportunity presents itself. • This cat's atypically short, "bobbed" tail is well suited to the shrubby and forested areas in which it hunts, but the bobcat is highly adaptable and may even be seen close to residential areas. • Like most young cats, bobcat kittens are almost always at play. **Where found:** coniferous and deciduous forests, brushy areas, riparian areas and willow stands.

# American Black Bear

### *Ursus americanus*

**Length:** 4½–6 ft (tail 3–7 in)
**Shoulder height:** 3–4 ft
**Weight:** 88–595 lb

The black bear's pelage is most commonly black but varies to cinnamon brown and to honey blond, with a lighter-colored muzzle. It is an excellent climber, with long claws that are also excellent for digging. • This omnivore eats plant material and obtains protein from insects such as bees (often while on honey raids), scavenged meat or, rarely, hunting small rodents or young deer. • The black bear spends winter in a den, but the hibernation is not deep, and the bear may rouse from its torpor and exit the den on mild winter days. **Where found:** forests, swamps or shrub thickets.

# Grizzly Bear

### Ursus arctos

**Length:** 6–8½ ft (tail 3–7 in)
**Shoulder height:** 3–4 ft
**Weight:** 240–1160 lb

Knowing that grizzly bears are around, though they are rarely seen, makes camping in the woods a truly wild experience. A mother grizzly with cubs can be very dangerous; hikers are advised to practice bear avoidance techniques.
• Grizzlies have a prominent shoulder hump, a dished face, a pale yellow to dark brown pelage and long front claws, which are always visible. Plants and carrion make up most of their omnivorous diet. **Where found:** forests and riparian areas in valley bottoms to high alpine tundra; though reported in the northern Cascades, the only stable population is in the Selkirks. **Also known as:** brown bear.

# Gray Wolf

### Canis lupus

**Length:** 4½–6½ ft (tail 14–20 in)
**Shoulder height:** 26–38 in
**Weight:** 57–170 lb

The hauntingly beautiful howl of the wolf is a unique and vital wilderness sound, but it has not always been appreciated; this animal was exterminated as vermin from much of its range. • Wolf packs have a strong social hierarchy with a dominant (alpha) male and female, which are often the only breeding pair in the pack. • Wolves have gray, white or occasionally black coats. They have a thicker, wider muzzle than coyotes and hold their tails high when running. **Where found:** a variety of habitats in remote wilderness areas in northeastern Washington. **Also known as:** timber wolf.

# Coyote

## *Canis latrans*

**Length:** 3½–4½ ft (tail 12–16 in)
**Shoulder height:** 23–26 in
**Weight:** 18–44 lb

Occasionally forming loose packs and joining in spirited yipping choruses, coyotes are intelligent, versatile hunter-scavengers and can best be described as opportunistic omnivores. They have been observed fishing or even engaging the help of a hunting badger to catch ground squirrels. • The size of an average dog, the coyote shares many characteristics that we appreciate in the domestic canine but accompanies only fellow pack members. **Where found:** mixed and coniferous forests, meadows, agricultural lands and suburban areas; almost every valley and most cities host a population of coyotes.

# Gray Fox

## *Urocyon cinereoargenteus*

**Length:** 30–43 in (tail 11–17 in)
**Shoulder height:** 14–15 in
**Weight:** 7½–13 lb

Preferring rocky, shrub-covered and forested terrain, and avoiding populated areas, the mainly nocturnal gray fox is rarely seen, unless you know where and when to look for it. • Most remarkable is this fox's ability to climb trees—the only member of the dog family able to do so—to escape danger, pursue birds or find egg-filled nests. It may even use a high tree-hollow for a den. • The gray fox's fur is shorter and denser than that of the red fox. **Where found:** open forests, shrub lands and rocky areas; along the western portion of Oregon to the coast.

# Kit Fox

### *Vulpes macrotis*

**Length:** 24–33 in (tail 9–13 in)
**Shoulder height:** 12 in
**Weight:** 3–6 lb

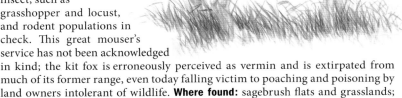

This housecat-sized fox does a great service to farmers and rural residents in keeping insect, such as grasshopper and locust, and rodent populations in check. This great mouser's service has not been acknowledged in kind; the kit fox is erroneously perceived as vermin and is extirpated from much of its former range, even today falling victim to poaching and poisoning by land owners intolerant of wildlife. **Where found:** sagebrush flats and grasslands; southeastern Oregon.

# Red Fox

### *Vulpes vulpes*

**Length:** 3–3½ ft (tail 14–17 in)
**Shoulder height:** 15 in
**Weight:** 8–15 lb

The red fox is a talented mouser with high-pouncing antics that are much more cat-like than dog-like. The entertaining, extroverted behavior and noble good looks of the red fox have landed it roles in many fairy tales, fables and native legends. • The red fox is typically a vivid reddish orange, but its coat can have darker color phases with dark fur across the back and shoulders, or it can be almost entirely black with silver-tipped hairs. The tip of its elegant, bushy tail, however, is always white. **Where found:** open, grassy habitats with brushy shelter, riparian areas and forest edges; avoids dense forests.

# Gray Whale

### *Eschrichtius robustus*

**Length:** average 45 ft; up to 50 ft
**Weight:** average 35 tons; up to 45 tons

The sole member of the gray whale family, this baleen whale lacks the significant throat pleating of the rorqual whales. Its gray skin is covered with a speckling of barnacles and carries large communities of other organisms, such as whale lice, along for the ride. • The gray whale is famous for its lengthy migrations that take it between the Arctic seas in summer and the Mexican coast in winter, thrilling whale watchers along the entire Pacific Coast as it passes by. **Where found:** generally coastal waters, as it migrates close to shore. **Also known as:** devilfish, mussel-digger, scrag whale.

# Minke Whale

### *Balaenoptera acutorostrata*

**Length:** average 27 ft; up to 35 ft
**Weight:** average 10 tons; up to 15 tons

Smallest of the rorquals—baleen whales with throats of pleated, expandable skin—the minke whale is occasionally seen in our waters, but it spends little time at the water's surface, so a fleeting glimpse is a lucky one. • The minke whale has been one of the more heavily hunted of the baleen whales since the 1980s, when larger whale populations had already collapsed. **Where found:** open water, sometimes in bays, inlets and estuaries; migrates seasonally between warm and cold waters. **Also known as:** piked whale, sharp-headed finner, little finner, lesser finback, lesser rorqual.

# Fin Whale

### *Balaenoptera physalus*

**Length:** average 70 ft; up to 89 ft
**Weight:** average 80 tons; up to 140 tons

When this long, sleek giant swims leisurely and gracefully along the surface of the water, its tall, narrow, dense blow reaches up to 20 ft high and is very noticeable on the horizon, but the fin whale does not show its fluke when beginning a dive. • Although these whales are found singly or in pairs, but more often in pods of 3–7 individuals, on occasion, several pods have been observed in a small area, creating concentrations of as many as 50 animals. • Fin whales are exceptionally fast movers and have been clocked at 20 mph in short bursts. **Where found:** offshore.

# Humpback Whale

### *Magaptera novaeangliae*

**Length:** average 45 ft; up to 62 ft
**Weight:** average 30 tons; up to 53 tons

The haunting songs of humpbacks can last from a few minutes to a few hours or even be epic, days-long concerts; they have inspired both scientists and artists and reach out to the imaginations of many people who listen and wonder what these great creatures are saying. • These rorquals employ a unique hunting strategy: they make a bubble net to round their prey into a tight cluster, thereby obtaining a food-dense gulpful. **Where found:** off our shores in summer; migrate in winter to the waters off Mexico or Costa Rica, some to Hawaii, to mate and calve.

# Orca

### *Orcinus orca*

**Length:** average 28 ft; up to 32 ft
**Weight:** average 7½ tons; up to 11 tons

Few people would not recognize this iconic creature that is found around the world. It is revered in legend and as a totem by Native Americans, celebrated by enthusiastic whale watchers and, unfortunately, cheered on for entertainment in captivity. • Researchers have identified 3 distinct types of killer whale along the Pacific coast: transients, residents and offshore types. Transients and residents differ in many ways, including home range size, morphology, hunting preferences and social behavior; offshore types are similar to residents but range farther from the coast. Residents are less commonly observed in our area. **Where found:** cool coastal waters, inshore and offshore. **Also known as:** killer whale.

# Short-beaked Common Dolphin

### *Delphinus delphis*

**Length:** average 6½ ft; up to 8½ ft
**Weight:** average 170 lb; up to 300 lb

Brilliant acrobatics accompany the thrill of having a group of common dolphins swim alongside your boat. They love to bow-ride (riding the momentum of the current made under the bow of a swift-moving boat) and can occur in very large groups of 50 up to 1000 individuals. • The long-beaked common dolphin (*D. capensis*) is very similar both physically and behaviorally to the short-beaked, but a trained eye can observe the characteristic distinctions. **Where found:** offshore along the coast.

# Risso's Dolphin

### *Grampus griseus*

**Length:** average 10 ft; up to 13 ft
**Weight:** average 880 lb; up to 1100 lb

Risso's dolphins have an interesting social behavior of scratching and biting at each other, leaving white scars all over their bodies—old individuals become so scarred that they appear almost completely white. They can also become scarred from being stung by large squid, their preferred prey. • Off our shores, they are typically observed as solitary individuals or in pairs, but they can occur in large herds, from 25 to several hundred, and become quite engaged in play sessions of breaching, spy-hopping, lob-tailing and flipper and fluke slapping. **Where found:** deep, offshore waters.

# Pacific White-sided Dolphin

### *Lagenorhynchus obliquidens*

**Length:** average 7 ft; up to 8 ft
**Weight:** average 210 lb; up to 400 lb

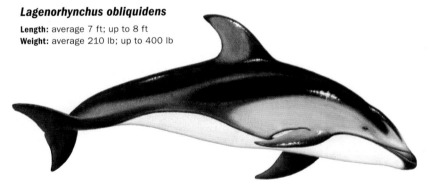

Whale watchers lucky enough to see Pacific white-sided dolphins often get some additional bonus entertainment from these highly acrobatic animals: breaching, somersaulting and bow-riding, seemingly very excited at the opportunity to show off. • Dolphins can focus their vision above and below water and often take a closer look at people by jumping alongside the boat or lifting their heads above the water's surface. **Where found:** open ocean; increased observations in coastal and sheltered waters, especially on the inside straits between islands and the mainland. **Also known as:** lag, Pacific striped dolphin, white-striped dolphin, hook-finned dolphin.

# Northern Elephant Seal

### *Mirounga angustirostris*

**Length:** *Male:* 12–16 ft; *Female:* 7–12 ft
**Weight:** *Male:* up to 5070 lb; *Female:* 2000 lb

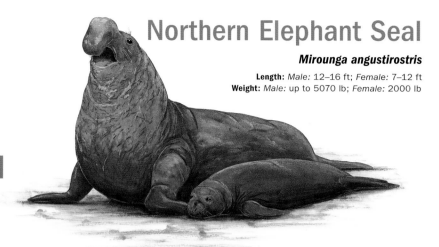

The northern elephant seal is the show-off of the seal family. It is the largest seal on our coast and dives to depths of up to 5000 ft in search of food, able to hold its breath for up to 80 minutes. A far-ranging male may cover 13,000 mi in migration between its northern feeding waters and winter breeding and molting beaches in California and Mexico, and spend more than 250 days at sea. • Both sexes sport the large snout, but that of the adult male is a pendulous, foot-long "trunk" that produces impressive rattling snorts. **Where found:** offshore, resting at the surface of the water.

# Harbor Seal

### *Phoca vitulina*

**Length:** 4–6 ft (tail 3½–4½ in)
**Weight:** 110–310 lb

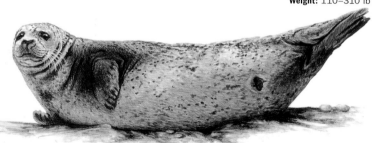

Year round, great colonies of harbor seals can be observed either basking in the day or sleeping at night on rocky shores and islands. Oftentimes during the day, individuals can be seen bobbing vertically in the water—the harbor seal cannot sleep at the surface in the manner in which sea otters can, but they can actually sleep underwater, going without breathing for up to 30 minutes. • They are shy of humans but do occasionally pop their heads up beside a canoe or kayak to investigate, usually making a quick retreat thereafter. **Where found:** bays and estuaries, intertidal sandbars and rocky shorelines along the coast.

# Northern Sea-Lion

### *Eumetopias jubatus*

**Length:** *Male:* 8½–11 ft; *Female:* 6–6½ ft
**Weight:** *Male:* up to 2200 lb; *Female:* 600–790 lb

Often seen in large groups, this seal cooperatively hunts for fish and forms dense
breeding and pupping colonies.
• Sea-lions are eared seals; the
ears are visible and are a good
identification feature in
comparison to
the hair seals
(harbor seal
and elephant seal),
whose ears are not visible
externally. • The California sea-lion (*Zalophus californianus*) tends to be more
common off Oregon's shores. **Where found:** coastal waters near rocky shores; may
rest in the water in a vertical position; prefer to be in the water during inclement
weather. **Also known as:** Steller sea-lion.

# Sea Otter

### *Enhydra lutris*

**Length:** 2½–5½ ft (tail 10–16 in)
**Weight:** 50–100 lb

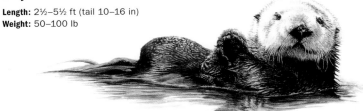

This buoyant otter lolls about on its back like a sunbather, floating in a manner us
humans can only somewhat achieve in the saltiest of seas. It can even sleep on the
water after anchoring itself in kelp beds, which are habitat for sea urchins, this
otter's favored prey. Reluctant to abandon the comfortable recline, the sea otter
grooms itself and dines while floating on its back, using tools such as rocks to
crack open the shells of its prey. **Where found:** shallow coastal areas with abundant
kelp beds; scattered populations along the West Coast; northern and western
coasts of the Olympic Peninsula.

# Northern River Otter

### *Lutra canadensis*

**Length:** 3½–4½ ft (tail 12–20 in)
**Weight:** 10–24 lb

The favorite sport of these frisky otters is sliding down wet, grassy riverbanks, even on snowy slopes in winter—look for their slide marks on the banks of rivers, lakes and ponds. • When they are not at play, they are engaged in the business of the hunt. These swift swimmers prey mainly upon aquatic species such as crustaceans, turtles, frogs and fish, but occasionally depredate birds' nests and eat small rodents. **Where found:** freshwater and saltwater habitats; lakes, ponds and streams and along the coast.

# American Marten

### *Martes americana*

**Length:** 20–26 in (tail 7–9 in)
**Weight:** 1–3 lb

An expert climber with semi-retractable claws, this forest dweller is quick and agile enough to catch arboreal squirrels. Although it spends most of its time on the ground, the marten often dens in a tree-hollow, where it raises its annual litter of 1–5 kits. • This animal is very elusive but not wary enough of the trapline, an ongoing threat even today. To see a marten in the deep forest is to know that you are in true wilderness. **Where found:** old-growth boreal and montane coniferous forests of spruce and fir with numerous dead trunks, branches and leaf cover for its rodent prey. **Also known as:** American sable, pine marten.

# Fisher

### *Martes pennanti*

**Length:** 2½–4 ft (tail 12–16 in)
**Weight:** 4½–12 lb

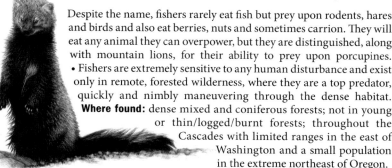

Despite the name, fishers rarely eat fish but prey upon rodents, hares and birds and also eat berries, nuts and sometimes carrion. They will eat any animal they can overpower, but they are distinguished, along with mountain lions, for their ability to prey upon porcupines. • Fishers are extremely sensitive to any human disturbance and exist only in remote, forested wilderness, where they are a top predator, quickly and nimbly maneuvering through the dense habitat. **Where found:** dense mixed and coniferous forests; not in young or thin/logged/burnt forests; throughout the Cascades with limited ranges in the east of Washington and a small population in the extreme northeast of Oregon.

# Short-tailed Weasel

### Mustela erminea

**Length:** 8½–13 in (tail 1½–3½ in)
**Weight:** 1½–4 oz

Although relatively common, the short-tailed weasel will not linger for any admiring observers; a spontaneous encounter with this curious creature will reveal its extraordinary speed and agility as it quickly escapes from view. • The short-tailed weasel is a voracious nocturnal hunter of mice and voles. Its coat is white in winter, but the tail is black-tipped year round. **Where found:** coniferous or mixed forests; in summer it may often be found in the alpine tundra, where it hunts on rockslides and talus slopes. **Also known as:** ermine, stoat.

# Long-tailed Weasel

### Mustela frenata

**Length:** 11–16½ in (tail 4½–11½ in)
**Weight:** 3–14 oz

Following the tracks of the long-tailed weasel on a snow-covered meadow offers good insight into the curious and energetic nature of this animal. Seemingly distracted from walking in a straight line, it continuously zigs and zags to investigate everything that catches its attention. • The long-tailed weasel feeds on small rodents, birds, insects, reptiles, amphibians and, occasionally, fruits and berries. Like other true weasels, it turns white in winter, but the tip of its tail remains black. **Where found:** aspen parklands, intermontane valleys and open forests.

# American Mink

### Mustela vison

**Length:** 18–28 in (tail 5–8½ in)
**Weight:** 1–3 lb

The mink's partially webbed feet make it an excellent swimmer, and it is capable of diving down to 10 ft in pursuit of fish. Its thick, dark brown to blackish, oily fur insulates its body from extremely cold water. • Mink travel along established hunting routes, often along shorelines, rarely passing a prey opportunity and stashing any surplus kills in temporary dens that are typically dug into riverbanks, beneath rock piles or in evacuated muskrat lodges. **Where found:** shorelines of lakes, marshes and streams; forests and grasslands in the foothills.

# Wolverine

### *Gulo gulo*

**Length:** 28–43 in (tail 7–10 in)
**Weight:** 15–35 lb

A large member of the weasel family, the wolverine looks like a small, frazzled bear. It has a poor reputation because of its occasional habit of raiding unoccupied wilderness cabins, eating the edible contents and spraying any leftovers with a foul-smelling musk from its anal musk gland…plenty of incentive to lock your cabin tight! • Its wild prey includes marmots, ground squirrels, gophers, mice, insects and berries, and it will scavenge carrion. **Where found:** remote, wooded foothills and mountains; alpine tundra in summer, lower elevations in winter; northern Washington and Cascade Mountains. **Also known as:** glutton, skunk bear.

# American Badger

### *Taxidea taxus*

**Length:** 25–35 in (tail 5–6½ in)
**Weight:** 11–24 lb

Equipped with huge claws and strong forelimbs, the badger is an efficient digger, able to excavate a den up to 30 ft long. Abandoned dens provide shelters and hibernacula for many creatures, from coyotes to black widow spiders. • The badger's powerful jaws, long teeth and aggressive defense tactics make it a formidable fighter. It preys mostly on burrowing mammals such as ground squirrels and other rodents. **Where found:** low-elevation fields, meadows, grasslands, fence lines and ditches; avoids forests but will visit alpine areas in summer in search of prey; throughout the eastern ½ of Washington and Oregon.

# Striped Skunk

### *Mephitis mephitis*

**Length:** 22–32 in (tail 8–14 in)
**Weight:** 4–9½ lb

Only the great horned owl, a regular predator of this small mammal, is undeterred by the odor of the striped skunk. Butylmercaptan is responsible for the stink of the skunk's musk. If sprayed into the eyes of an attacker, it can also cause burning, tearing and even temporary blindness. • When undisturbed, this skunk is a quiet, reclusive omnivore, feeding mostly on insects, worms, bird eggs, reptiles and amphibians, grains, green vegetation and berries. **Where found:** low-elevation streamside woodlands, hardwood groves, semi-open areas, brushy grasslands and valleys; also in urban environments, where it will raid gardens and garbage bins.

# Western Spotted Skunk

## *Spilogale gracilis*

**Length:** 13–23 in (tail 4–8 in)
**Weight:** 1–2 lb

When threatened, the western spotted skunk
stamps its feet in alarm or makes short lunges
at its perceived attacker, which will pay the smelly
price if it ignores the warning. Although this assault is
no laughing matter, the posture this small mammal assumes in order to spray is
comical—the skunk literally performs a handstand, arches its back so that its back-
side and tail face forward above its head, and then walks toward its assailant while
spraying it. • When not performing such feats of showmanship, this nocturnal
skunk feeds mostly on insects, primarily grasshoppers and crickets. **Where found:**
woodlands, riparian zones, rocky areas, open grasslands or scrublands and farmlands; the west and extreme southeast of Washington and throughout Oregon.

# Ringtail

## *Bassariscus astutus*

**Length:** 25–32 in (tail 12–17 in)
**Weight:** 1½–2½ lb

A member of the raccoon family, the ringtail
is reminiscent of a cat, even in the way it
hunts by stalking and pouncing upon its prey
of small mammals, reptiles and amphibians. The ringtail's omnivorous diet also
includes insects, bird eggs and nestlings, carrion and fruit. • Cacomistle, an
alternate name for this animal, is derived from the language of the Mexican
Nahuatl people and means "half mountain lion," furthering the cat comparisons.
**Where found:** rocky slopes, cliffs and canyons in the extreme southwest of Oregon.
**Also known as:** cacomistle, civet cat, miner's cat, ring-tailed cat.

# Northern Raccoon

## *Procyon lotor*

**Length:** 26–38 in (tail 7½–16 in)
**Weight:** 12–31 lb

A garbage container is no match for the raccoon's
curiosity, persistence and problem-solving abilities,
making your trash and the garden goldfish pond prime
targets for midnight food raids in urban areas. In this animal's natural habitat of
forest streams, lakes and ponds, an omnivorous diet of clams, frogs, fish, bird eggs
and nestlings, berries, nuts and insects is more than ample. Raccoons build up their
fat reserves during the warm months to sustain themselves throughout winter.
**Where found:** low-elevation riparian areas; the edges of forests and wetlands.

# Porcupine

### *Erethizon dorsatum*

**Length:** 21–37 in (tail 5½–9 in)
**Weight:** 8–40 lb

A porcupine cannot throw its 30,000 or so quills but delivers them into the flesh of an attacker with a quick flick of the tail. The quills are dangerous but attractive, common in traditional Native American beadwork. • This excellent tree climber fills its vegetarian diet with forbs, shrubs and the sugary cambium of trees; an insatiable craving for salt occasionally drives it to gnaw on rubber tires, wooden ax handles, hiking boots and even toilet seats! • This slow-moving nocturnal creature is a common roadkill victim. **Where found:** coniferous and mixed forests, open tundra and even rangelands.

# Mountain Beaver

### *Aplodontia rufa*

**Length:** 12–18 in (tail ½–2 in)
**Weight:** ½–3 lb

Capable of swimming only short distances, this rodent prefers to climb trees, and rather than build an aquatic den, it burrows tunnels and nesting chambers into dry ground. • The mountain beaver feeds primarily on sword ferns and bracken ferns, which are toxic to most other rodents, but also forages on seedlings and the cambium of saplings; the male eats large amounts of red alder leaves in fall. **Where found:** deciduous forests with plenty of shrubs, forbs and young trees; from near sea level to the treeline; throughout western Washington and Oregon.

# Beaver

### *Castor canadensis*

**Length:** 3–4 ft (tail 11–21 in)
**Weight:** 35–66 lb

The loud slap of a beaver's tail on water warns of intruders. A beaver can remain submerged under water for 15 minutes, and its tail is an extremely effective propulsion device for swimming and diving. • Beavers use their long, continuously growing incisors to cut down trees in short order, and their strong jaws can drag a 20-lb piece of wood. • Oregon adopted this industrious species as the state animal in 1969. **Where found:** lakes, ponds, marshes and slow-flowing rivers and streams at most elevations with ample vegetation.

# Nutria

### *Myocastor coypus*

**Length:** 2–4½ ft (tail 12–18 in)
**Weight:** 5–25 lb

This South American species was
introduced to be farmed for its fur.
The venture was not profitable, and
many animals escaped and are now part of the ecology with significant disturbance
to some native species. Ironically, our beavers were introduced to Argentina,
where similar ecological upset has occurred. • Nutrias eat wetland vegetation and
den in a deep dugout in a bank. **Where found:** rivers, lakes and marshes with
abundant emergent or submerged vegetation and that do not freeze over in winter;
Puget Trough and Willamette Valley; Pacific coast excluding the Olympic Peninsula.
**Also known as:** coypu.

# Common Muskrat

### *Ondatra zibethicus*

**Length:** 18–24 in (tail 7½–11 in)
**Weight:** 1½–3½ lb

Although they have similar habitats and
behaviors, the beaver and the common
muskrat are not closely related. The muskrat does sport large incisors that it uses to
cut through a vast array of thick vegetation, particularly cattails and bulrushes, and
it makes a partially submerged den similar to that of a beaver. A muskrat den
provides nesting spots for many geese and ducks as well as important shelter for
other rodents when the muskrat moves house. **Where found:** low-elevation sloughs,
lakes, marshes and streams with plenty of cattails, rushes and open water.

# Bushy-tailed Woodrat

### *Neotoma cinerea*

**Length:** 11–18 in (tail 4½–9 in)
**Weight:** 3–18 oz

Woodrats are infamous for
collecting objects, whether natural
or man-made and whether useful or
merely decorative accents, for their large, messy nests. Twigs, bones,
pinecones, bottle caps, rings, pens and coins are picked up as this rodent scouts
for treasures, often trading an object in its mouth for the next, more attractive
item it encounters. A woodrat's nest is often more easily found than the woodrat
itself. **Where found:** rocky outcroppings, shrublands, caves and mine shafts; from
grasslands to alpine zones. **Also known as:** packrat, trade rat.

# Norway Rat

### *Rattus norvegicus*

**Length:** 12–18 in (tail 4½–9 in)
**Weight:** 7–17 oz

Native to Europe and Asia, the Norway rat came to North America as a stow-away on ships back around 1775. It is mainly associated with human settlements, feeding on cereal grains, fruits, vegetation and garbage and basically making a nuisance of itself—another example of an introduced species becoming a reviled pest, though only surviving in a non-native environment. • Captive-bred rats have aided scientific research in many fields. **Where found:** urban areas, farmyards and garbage dumps. **Also known as:** brown rat, common rat, sewer rat, water rat.

# Deer Mouse

### *Peromyscus maniculatus*

**Length:** 5½–8½ in (tail 2–4 in)
**Weight:** ¾–1¼ oz

Abundant deer mice are seedeaters, but they will also eat insects, spiders, caterpillars, fungi, flowers and berries. Deer mice are in turn important prey for many other animals; thus they must be prolific breeders to maintain their population. A litter of 4–9 young leaves the nest after 3–5 weeks, and the mice are sexually mature 1–2 weeks later. Less than 5% of deer mice survive a complete year. **Where found:** most dry habitats; grasslands, shrublands and forests; also find ample shelter and food in human settings.

# House Mouse

### *Mus musculus*

**Length:** 5–8 in (tail 2½–4 in)
**Weight:** ½–¾ oz

This familiar mouse can be found throughout most of North America. Like the Norway rat, it arrived as a stow-away on ships from Europe, quickly spreading across the continent alongside European settlers. • The house mouse is nocturnal in habit and may be responsible for gnawing the labels off the canned soup stored in your cupboards! Its pelage is brownish to blackish gray with gray undersides. **Where found:** usually associated with human settlements, including urban houses, garages, farmyards, garbage dumps and granaries.

# Montane Vole

### Microtus montanus

**Length:** 5–7½ in (tail 1–2½ in)
**Weight:** ½–1¾ oz

Montane voles are one of the most abundant
small mammals in many parts of our area.
Favorable environmental conditions may allow montane
voles to reproduce to densities of up to 2500 voles per acre! There are
several species of vole, but if you see a vole in montane habitat, chances are high
that it is a montane vole. • The montane vole is a prey species for owls, hawks,
weasels and coyotes. **Where found:** mountain meadows, valleys and some arid
sagebrush communities.

# Pacific Jumping Mouse

### Zapus trinotatus

**Length:** 8–10 in (tail 4–6 in)
**Weight:** ¾–1 oz

These jumping mice are
not only long jumpers
(covering nearly 1 yard
in a single bound) but long sleepers as well. Pacific jumping mice hibernate from
October until April, waking *en masse* when the rise in soil temperatures stirs
them from their underground chambers. • They feed on fungi, seeds, berries and
tender vegetation as well as insects in spring. **Where found:** dense plant cover,
stream sides, thickets, wet sedge meadows, most fields and certain woodlands;
common where skunk cabbage grows; mountains from valley floors to above
treeline.

# Great Basin Pocket Mouse

### Perognathus parvus

**Length:** 6–8 in (tail 3½–4½ in)
**Weight:** ½–1 oz

Pocket mice tend to sit with their large
hind feet centered below themselves
and their small forelegs held up.
They move with either a slow
walk or a peculiar 4-footed hop.
They are very fond of dust baths, rolling and digging in sandy areas and brushing
their fur afterwards, likely to rid themselves of parasites and to keep their fur well
groomed. They will also invert their cheek pouches and clean them against the
sand. **Where found:** arid, sparsely vegetated flatlands east of the Cascades.

71

# Ord's Kangaroo Rat

### *Dipodomys ordii*

**Length:** 9–11 in (tail 5½–6½ in)
**Weight:** 1½–3½ oz

Powerful hind legs and a long, muscular tail give this endearing little creature the ability to leap 6–8 ft in a single hop. • Mainly a nocturnal granivore, it forages in the sand for seeds and the occasional plant or insect by night, and rests in its short, sandy burrow by day. It rarely drinks water, obtaining needed liquids from food and internally recycled wastes. **Where found:** sandy, semi-desert grasslands and sagebrush sites; open and disturbed areas with sandy soils or dunes; eastern Oregon extending just past the border into south-central Washington.

# Northern Pocket Gopher

### *Thomomys talpoides*

**Length:** 7½–10 in (tail 1½–3 in)
**Weight:** 2½–7½ oz

The northern pocket gopher is a well-adapted subterranean rodent. Its feet have naked soles and are equipped with long front claws for digging; furred lips extend over the long incisor teeth, preventing dirt from entering its mouth while eating and digging; fur-lined cheek pouches store succulent roots, tubers and green plants. Although it spends most of its life underground, the northern pocket gopher occasionally tunnels to the surface at night to feed, leaving distinct dirt mounds. **Where found:** mountain meadows, fields, shrublands, grasslands and open pine forests of the West.

# Townsend's Chipmunk

### *Tamias townsendii*

**Length:** 8½–14 in (tail 3½–6 in)
**Weight:** 1½–4 oz

Townsend's chipmunks run across the beach and through the coast forests with their tails held high like a proud flag. They dig burrows at the base of a tree or in a rock crevice and hibernate only in the cold, higher elevations, staying active year round near the coast. • The smaller, brightly striped yellow-pine chipmunk (*T. amoenus*) is common from the Cascades east and on the Olympic Peninsula. **Where found:** driftwood beaches, dense hardwood and mixed forests; fern-filled, moist coniferous forests; from sea level to 6500 ft.

# Yellow-bellied Marmot

### *Marmota flaviventris*

**Length:** 19–26 in (tail 5–7½ in)
**Weight:** 3½–10 lb

Yellow-bellied marmots live in colonies and excavate burrows under rocky terrain to hide from the elements and from predators such as eagles and foxes. A loud chirp of varying intensities alerts the colony to impending dangers.
• Marmots spend their lazy days eating, sleeping and raising young, basking in the summer sun or hibernating in winter. • Endemic to the Olympic Peninsula is the Olympic marmot (*M. olympus*). **Where found:** rocky talus slopes and outcroppings among grassy vegetation; rocky, subalpine, semi-open areas and arid grasslands; from the Cascades east. **Also known as:** rockchuck.

# Golden-mantled Ground Squirrel

### *Spermophilus lateralis*

**Length:** 11–13 in (tail 3½–5 in)
**Weight:** 6–12 oz

A familiar campground resident, this ground squirrel is frequently referred to as a large chipmunk because of somewhat similar striping. The golden-mantled ground squirrel often has its cheek pouches crammed with seeds.
• With slightly overlapping ranges, the more common ground squirrel along the west coast is the California ground squirrel (*S. beecheyi*), lacking the distinct stripes of its golden-mantled relative. • The Cascade golden-mantled ground squirrel (*S. saturatus*) is endemic to the Cascade Mountains of Washington and southwestern British Columbia. **Where found:** montane and subalpine forests with rocky outcroppings or talus slopes; possibly open coniferous zones and high deserts.

# Western Gray Squirrel

### *Sciurus griseus*

**Length:** 18–25 in (tail 9½–12 in)
**Weight:** 1–2 lb

In true squirrel fashion, western gray squirrels are so nuts about nuts—acorns, hazelnuts, pine nuts—that they store them in forked tree branches, under fallen logs or underground, where they often germinate, making this squirrel a fortuitous gardener. • Eastern gray and eastern fox squirrels (*S. carolinensis* and *S. niger*) are both introduced species that occur in western gray squirrel territory. **Where found:** woodlands, especially oak; sea level to low elevations of west-central Washington south through Oregon. **Also known as:** California gray squirrel, Columbian gray squirrel, silver gray squirrel.

# Douglas's Squirrel

### *Tamiasciurus douglassii*

**Length:** 11–14 in (tail 4–6 in)
**Weight:** 5–11 oz

This noisy inhabitant of the coniferous coastal rainforest has a wide repertoire of chattering calls. With an insatiable appetite for conifer cones, Douglas's squirrel tirelessly leaps from branch to branch and tree to tree, nipping off and dropping cones to the ground for later collection. • The red squirrel (*T. hudsonicus*) is a common visitor of backyards and town parks with large, old trees and is also found in the boreal and mixed forests of the Selkirks and south into Oregon. **Where found:** coniferous coastal rainforest and Cascade forests; western Washington and Oregon. **Also known as:** chickaree.

# Northern Flying Squirrel

### *Glaucomys sabrinus*

**Length:** 9½–15 in (tail 4–7 in)
**Weight:** 2½–6½ oz

Long flaps of skin stretched between the fore and hind limbs and a broad, flattened tail allow the nocturnal northern flying squirrel to glide swiftly from tree to tree, with extreme glides of up to 110 yards! • This flying squirrel plays an important role in forest ecology because it digs up and eats truffles, spreading around the fruiting body of the beneficial ectomycorrhizal fungus. **Where found:** primarily old-growth coniferous forests; sometimes aspen and cottonwood forests; throughout much of our region, but particularly in western mountain ranges.

# Pygmy Rabbit

### *Brachylagus idahoensis*

**Length:** 10–12 in (tail 1–1½ in)
**Weight:** 10–15 oz

This tiny, native rabbit favors desert or semi-desert conditions, of which habitat type it is a keystone species; it is unable to survive elsewhere, and many other species are dependant upon its presence as prey or for use of its abandoned burrows. • Unlike other native rabbits, the pygmy excavates its own burrow in the hard soil of sagebrush flats. The bitter sagebrush leaves are the major component of this rabbit's diet. **Where found:** dense stands of sagebrush or rabbitbrush; desert and semi-desert areas of the Great Basin area between the Rocky Mountains and the Cascades of Oregon.

# Brush Rabbit

### *Sylvilagus bachmani*

**Length:** 11–15 in (tail ½–1½ in)
**Weight:** 1–2 lb

This tiny rabbit is typically seen at dawn and
dusk feeding on tender vegetation. Capable of
up to 5 litters of 3–4 young per litter in a single year,
the brush rabbit maintains its population by being prolific.
Small ears (about 2 in long) are more suitable to the cool coastal climate, and the
lack of snowfall removes the need for this rabbit to camouflage white in winter.
**Where found:** areas with plenty of brush cover; western Oregon.

# Mountain Cottontail

### *Sylvilagus nuttallii*

**Length:** 13–16 in (tail 1–2½ in)
**Weight:** 1½–2½ lb

Mountain cottontails hide out during the day in
shallow burrows, called forms, covered by impen-
etrable vegetation, or they hide in rock crevices.
Their secretive nature is owing to their many predators,
which include bobcats, coyotes and birds of prey. As well,
the adults do not camouflage white in winter; thus, they
become even more reclusive but do not hibernate. **Where found:**
wherever there is cover in brush, rocky areas or buildings; throughout eastern
Washington and Oregon. **Also known as:** Nuttall's cottontail.

# Snowshoe Hare

### *Lepus americanus*

**Length:** 15–21 in (tail 2 in)
**Weight:** 2–3½ lb

Extremely well adapted to surviving harsh alpine winters, the
snowshoe hare has large hind feet that allow it to move across
deep snow without sinking in, and the white pelage in
winter camouflages it. If detected by a predator, the hare
explodes into a running zigzag pattern in its flight
for cover, sometimes reaching speeds of 32 mph.
• Populations of the snowshoe hare, its winter food
sources of willow and alder and its main predator,
the lynx, are closely inter-related and cyclical.
**Where found:** brushy, second-growth forests.
**Also known as:** varying hare.

# White-tailed Jackrabbit

### *Lepus townsendii*

**Length:** 21–25 in (tail 2½–4½ in)
**Weight:** 6½–12 lb

Unlike rabbits, which give birth to altricial young, hares give birth to precocial young—fully furred, open eyed and able to move about. Rather than hide from danger, hares, capable of running 45 mph in short spurts, try to outrun predators. • The white-tailed jackrabbit's fur turns white in winter, with just black-tipped ears. The black-tailed jackrabbit (*L. californicus*), with an overlapping range in eastern Oregon but barely crossing into Washington, does not turn white in winter. **Where found:** grasslands and open areas, entering woodlands for winter shelter but avoiding forests; eastern half of both states. **Also known as:** prairie hare.

# Pika

### *Ochotona princeps*

**Length:** 6–8½ in
**Weight:** 4–6½ oz

The busy pika scurries in and out of rocky crevices to issue its warning *PEEEK!* call and to gather large bundles of succulent grasses to dry on sun-drenched rocks and store for later consumption during winter, when it rarely leaves its shelter under the snow. In summer, it makes grassy nests within the rocks to have its young. • Although tail-less and with rounded ears, the pika is a close relative of rabbits and hares. **Where found:** rocky talus slopes and rocky fields at higher elevations. **Also known as:** cony.

# Little Brown Bat

### *Myotis lucifugus*

**Length:** 2½–4 in (tail 1–2 in)
**Wingspan:** 10 in (forearm 1½ in)
**Weight:** ¼ oz

On warm, calm summer nights, the skies are filled with shrill calls of bats, but the frequencies are beyond the range of our hearing. This bat is most commonly seen skimming over lakes, ponds and even swimming pools to get a quick drink or in pursuit of insects. • There are several species of mouse-eared bats (*Myotis* spp.) in our area, but they are generally indistinguishable from each other as they fly in dim light. **Where found:** roosts in buildings, barns, caves, rock crevices, hollow trees and under tree bark; hibernates in buildings, caves and mine adits.

# Hoary Bat

### *Lasiurus cinereus*

**Length:** 4–6 in (tail 1½–2½ in)
**Wingspan:** 16 in (forearm 1¾–2½ in)
**Weight:** 1–1¼ oz

This large, beautiful bat roosts in trees, not caves or buildings, and wraps its wings around itself for protection against the elements, its frosty-colored fur blending in amongst the mosses and lichens. The hoary bat also roosts in orchards, but it is an insectivore and does not damage fruit crops. At night, look for its large size and slow wingbeats over open terrain.
• The western red bat (*L. blossevillii*) is slightly smaller with reddish coloring and overlaps the western range of the hoary bat. **Where found:** near open areas; lakes near coniferous and deciduous forests.

# Silver-haired Bat

### *Lasionycteris noctivagans*

**Length:** 3½–4½ in (tail 1½–2 in)
**Wingspan:** 12 in (forearm 1½–2 in)
**Weight:** ¼–½ oz

Silver-haired bats take flight at dawn and dusk's twilights on feeding forays for moths and flies over open fields, water surfaces and treetops. • To conserve energy on cold days, they can lower their body temperature and metabolism and go into a state known as torpor. • These bats prefer to roost in trees. Small colonies of silver-haired bats may choose to hibernate in caves, mines or abandoned buildings. Females form nursery colonies in protected shelters such as tree cavities. **Where found:** roosts in cavities and crevices of old-growth trees but can adapt to parks, cities and farmlands.

# Big Brown Bat

### *Eptesicus fuscus*

**Length:** 3½–5½ in (tail 1–2½ in)
**Wingspan:** 13 in (forearm 1½–2 in)
**Weight:** ½–1 oz

An effective aerial hunter, the big brown bat's ultrasonic echolocation (80,000–40,000 Hz) can detect flying insects up to 16 ft away. It flies above water, around streetlights or over agricultural areas, hunting insects at dusk and dawn. • The big brown bat is not abundant but is frequently encountered because of its tendency to roost in man-made structures. It has been known to change hibernation sites mid-winter, a time when it is extremely rare to spot a bat. **Where found:** in and around man-made structures; occasionally roosts in hollow trees and rock crevices.

# Western Pipistrelle

### *Pipistrellus hesperus*

**Length:** 2½–3½ in (tail 1–1¼ in)
**Wingspan:** 7½–8½ in (forearm 1–1¼ in)
**Weight:** ¼ oz

The smallest bat in the U.S. is the western pipistrelle. It is also quite delicate, with a weak, erratic flight style, making it unable to fly in strong wind. The jerky flight of its European counterparts gave it the name "flittermouse" (or *fledermaus* in German). This is one of the few bat species that can be seen active at midday. • The contrasting black "mask," wings and legs against blond fur make this bat distinctively attractive. **Where found:** arid regions with rocky or scrubby areas; sometimes close to cities; southeastern Washington and eastern Oregon.

# Townsend's Big-eared Bat

### *Plecotus townsendii*

**Length:** 3½–4½ in (tail 1–2½ in)
**Wingspan:** 11 in (forearm 1½–2 in)
**Weight:** ¼–½ oz

Endowed with relatively enormous ears about a third of its body length, these bats "see" the nighttime world through sound (though all bats have good eyesight, contrary to the blind-as-a-bat myth). Each species of bat is recognizable by the ultrasonic calls it produces, but special equipment is needed to identify bat calls. Bats can hear frequencies as much as 200 times higher than our ears can hear. **Where found:** open areas near coniferous forests; hibernate deep within caves. **Also known as:** western big-eared bat.

# Coast Mole

### *Scapanus orarius*

**Length:** 5½–7 in (tail 1–1½ in)
**Weight:** 2–3 oz

Moles are the backhoes and bulldozers of the mammalian world, keeping soil healthy by aerating it, encouraging water absorption and circulating nutrients. A deposit of subsurface soil above ground is commonly referred to as a molehill, typically 7 in high and abundant between October and March for this species. • The coast mole mainly eats earthworms. **Where found:** meadows, deciduous woodlands and brushy areas; along the western half of both states extending through northern Oregon. **Also known as:** Pacific mole.

# Vagrant Shrew

### *Sorex vagrans*

**Length:** 3½–5 in (tail 1½ in)
**Weight:** ¼ oz

Several species of shrew are found
in various ranges and habitats,
but the vagrant shrew is found
throughout most of both
states. Shrew species are
almost indistinguishable
in the field. • The vagrant
shrew eats a variety of
insects, earthworms, spiders, snails, slugs, carrion
and some vegetation as it scrounges about in the
understory. **Where found:** forested regions with nearby
water; sometimes along the edge of brooks and willow
banks.

# Virginia Opossum

### *Didelphis virginiana*

**Length:** 27–33 in (tail 12–14 in)
**Weight:** 2½–3½ lb

Contrary to most children's stories in which
opossums are portrayed hanging by their
prehensile tails, the Virginia opossum
rarely assumes this posture, though it does
climb and den in trees. It is a marsupial
closely related to kangaroos and koalas.
• The trick of playing dead, a role this
actor is famous for, is performed when
attacked in hopes of being left alone.
This is where the expression
"playing possum" comes from.
However, playing dead has
unsuccessful results against
cars, which are this slow-moving
nocturnal creature's most common
assailant. **Where found:** moist woodlands or brushy areas near watercourses; western Washington and
Oregon.

# BIRDS

All birds are feathered, but not all fly. The most diverse class of vertebrates, birds are bipedal, warm-blooded and lay hard-shelled eggs. Some birds migrate south in the colder winter months and return north in spring. For this reason, Washington and Oregon have a different diversity of birds in summer than in winter. Many migrating birds fly as far south as Central and South America. These neotropical migrants are of concern to biologists and conservationists because pesticide use and decreasing habitat in these countries threaten the survival of many species. Education and increasing appreciation for wildlife may encourage solutions to this problem.

Waterfowl
pp. 82–87

Grouse-like Birds
p. 88

Diving Birds
pp. 89–90

Herons & Vultures
pp. 90–91

Birds of Prey
pp. 91–93

Rails & Cranes
p. 94

Shorebirds
pp. 94–98

Gulls, Terns & Alcids
pp. 99–101

Pigeons & Doves
p. 101

Owls
pp. 102–03

**Nighthawks & Swifts**
p. 104

**Hummingbirds & Kingfishers**
pp. 104–05

**Woodpeckers**
pp. 105–06

**Flycatchers**
pp. 106–07

**Shrikes & Vireos**
p. 108

**Jays & Crows**
pp. 108–10

**Larks & Swallows**
p. 110

**Chickadees & Nuthatches**
p. 111

**Wrens, Dippers & Kinglets**
pp. 112–13

**Robin & Wrentit**
p. 113

**Starlings & Waxwings**
p. 114

**Wood-warblers
& Tanagers**
pp. 114–16

**Sparrows
& Grosbeaks**
pp. 116–18

**Blackbirds
& Allies**
pp. 118–19

**Finch-like
Birds**
pp. 119–20

# Canada Goose

### *Branta canadensis*

**Length:** 35–45 in
**Wingspan:** 4½–6 ft

Canada geese mate for life and are devoted parents to their 2–11 goslings. Wild geese can be aggressivewhen defending their young or competing for food. Hissing sounds and low, outstretched necks are signs that you should give these birds some space.

• Geese graze on aquatic grasses and sprouts, and you can spot them tipping up to grab for aquatic roots and tubers. • The Canada goose was split into 2 species in 2004; the smaller subspecies has been renamed the cackling goose. **Where found:** along waterbodies; parks, marshes and croplands.

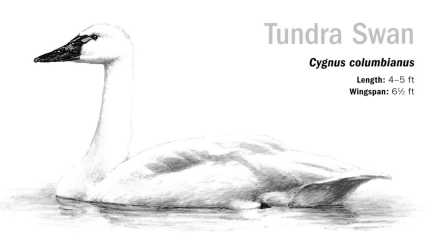

# Tundra Swan

### *Cygnus columbianus*

**Length:** 4–5 ft
**Wingspan:** 6½ ft

A wave of tundra swans flying overhead is a sight you will never forget as they migrate between breeding grounds in the Arctic and winter grounds along the Pacific Northwest coast. • These birds feed on aquatic plants, able to reach with their long necks and strong bills bottom-growing tubers and shoots that ducks and other geese are unable to access. Tundra swans have taken recent liking to more widely available waste grain in agricultural areas. **Where found:** shallow areas of lakes and wetlands, agricultural fields and flooded pastures in winter.

# Wood Duck

### *Aix sponsa*

**Length:** 15–20 in
**Wingspan:** 30 in

The forest-dwelling wood duck is equipped with fairly sharp claws for perching on branches and nesting in tree cavities, which may be 20–30 ft high. Shortly after hatching, the ducklings jump out of their nest cavity, often falling those 20–30 ft, but, like downy balls, they bounce upon landing and are seldom injured. A female wood duck often returns to the same nest site each year; being already familiar with potential threats at established nest sites may improve her brood's survival rate. **Where found:** swamps, ponds, marshes and lakeshores with wooded edges.

# Gadwall

### *Anas strepera*

**Length:** 18–22 in
**Wingspan:** 33 in

Gadwall numbers have recently reached record levels, with the North American population climbing to over 1.4 million breeding pairs in the 21st century. Both sexes of these medium-sized dabbling ducks are grayish brown overall with bold white wing patches, but males sport a black rump and undertail coverts, and females have orange and brown bills. • These ducks feed on a variety of aquatic plants and invertebrates and are typically found in deep water, farther from shore than other dabbling ducks. **Where found:** freshwater lakes or ponds; less common in brackish or saline ponds or estuaries.

# Mallard

### *Anas platyrhynchos*

**Length:** 20–28 in
**Wingspan:** 3 ft

The male mallard, with his shiny, green head and chestnut brown breast, is the classic wild duck, and this duck species is one of the only ones that really "quacks." • A grass nest is built on the ground or under a bush, where the female incubates 7–10 creamy, grayish or greenish white eggs. Mallards readily hybridize with a variety of other duck species, including barnyard ducks, often producing offspring with very peculiar plumages. **Where found:** lakes, wetlands, rivers, city parks, agricultural areas, sewage lagoons and even outdoor swimming pools; year round.

# Northern Pintail

### *Anas acuta*

**Length:** *Male:* 25–30 in;
*Female:* 20–22 in
**Wingspan:** 34 in

Its long neck and long, tapered tail give this dabbling duck a style of its own. This migrant is among the millions of waterfowl that visit the marshes, lakes and grain fields of the Pacific Flyway each year. Habitat management in our area has proven to be crucial to relieve the pressure on local croplands and to provide important staging and feeding grounds to northern pintails and many other ducks. **Where found:** shallow wetlands, flooded fields and lake edges.

# Green-winged Teal

***Anas crecca***

**Length:** 14 in
**Wingspan:** 23 in

Green-winged teals are the smallest of our dabbling ducks and weigh less than 1 lb. They are among the most widely hunted ducks and choose secluded breeding grounds. After breeding, males often undergo a partial migration before molting into duller "eclipse" plumage. These teals lose all of their flight feathers at once, rendering them flightless for a few weeks, during which they must avoid predators by hiding in thick vegetation or roosting in open water. **Where found:** various freshwater and estuarine habitats, favoring shallow marshes with low cover.

# Ring-necked Duck

***Aythya collaris***

**Length:** 14–18 in
**Wingspan:** 23–25 in

On a winter's walk around a quiet pond, you will likely encounter the ring-necked duck. It is common in western Washington and Oregon in winter and in the eastern half of the two states in summer or in migration, though some areas have year-round residents. • This duck is similar in appearance to the scaup, but notice the bill on the ring-neck and see how it might be more appropriately named the "ring-billed duck," especially because the ring on its neck is rarely visible. **Where found:** *Breeding:* shallow, permanent freshwater wetlands. *In migration:* small water bodies; prefers wooded or vegetated, slow-moving freshwater.

# Lesser Scaup

### Aythya affinis
**Length:** 15–18 in
**Wingspan:** 25 in

Two scaup species occur in our area, and their tricolor appearance makes these widespread diving ducks easy to recognize and remember. The lesser scaup has a smaller white inner wing stripe that changes to dull gray on its primaries, while the greater scaup (*A. marila*) has a larger white wing stripe that extends into the secondary flight feathers. The male lesser scaup has a purple, peaked head, while the greater scaup has a green, rounded head. **Where found:** lakes, open marshes and along slow-moving rivers; nests outside our area.

# Surf Scoter

### Melanitta perspicillata
**Length:** 17–21 in
**Wingspan:** 28–31 in

The surf scoter sits like a sturdy buoy on the waves of bays, inlets and large lakes. This bird breeds in Alaska and northern Canada and is well adapted for life on rough waters, spending winters just beyond the breaking surf on the Atlantic and Pacific coasts. • Although the surf scoter is the only scoter that breeds and overwinters exclusively on this continent, it is largely unstudied. **Where found:** bays and inlets along the coast; large, deep lakes and slow-moving rivers in the interior.

# Common Goldeneye

*Bucephala clangula*

**Length:** 16–20 in
**Wingspan:** 26 in

The typical common goldeneye spends its entire life in North America, dividing its time between breeding and nesting grounds in the boreal forests of Canada and Alaska and its winter territory in marine bays and estuaries along the Pacific and Atlantic coasts. In winter, female common goldeneyes fly farther south than males, and juvenile birds continue even farther south. Many of these birds also overwinter on large inland rivers, lakes and reservoirs, but numbers depend on food availability and open water. **Where found:** open water on lakes, large ponds and rivers.

# Common Merganser

*Mergus merganser*

**Length:** 22–27 in
**Wingspan:** 34 in

The common merganser must run along the surface of the water beating its heavy wings to gain sufficient lift to take off; once up and away, it flies arrow-straight and low over the water. • This large duck nests in a tree cavity, on a cliff ledge, in a large nest box or occasionally on the ground, usually close to water. • In winter, any source of open water with a fish-filled shoal will support good numbers of these skilled divers. **Where found:** large rivers and deep lakes.

# Ring-necked Pheasant

### *Phasianus colchicus*

**Length:** *Male:* 30–36 in; *Female:* 20–26 in
**Wingspan:** *Male:* 31 in; *Female:* 28 in

Since being introduced in the late 1800s, this Asian bird has had to endure many pressures. Its numbers have had to be continually replenished by hatchery-raised young, not only because it is hunted, but also because of diminished habitat, intensive farming practices and harsh winters. Unlike native grouse, the ring-necked pheasant lacks feathered legs and feet for insulation and cannot survive on native plants but depends on grain and corn crops. **Where found:** shrubby grasslands, urban parks, woodlots, hayfields and croplands on both sides of the Cascades.

# Ruffed Grouse

### *Bonasa umbellus*

**Length:** 15–19 in
**Wingspan:** 22 in

A low, booming sound echoing through the forest in spring is most likely being made by a male ruffed grouse "drumming" to announce his territory. Every spring, and occasionally in fall, the male grouse struts along a fallen log with his tail fanned and his neck feathers ruffed, beating the air periodically with accelerating wing strokes. • In winter, scales grow out along the sides of the ruffed grouse's feet, creating temporary "snowshoes." **Where found:** hardwood and mixed forests and riparian woodlands; young, second-growth stands with birch and aspen.

# California Quail

### *Callipepla californica*

**Length:** 10–11 in
**Wingspan:** 14 in

First introduced to our area in the 1800s, though largely absent from the coast, California quails are year-round residents in low-elevation brushy habitats and parks. They are seen scuttling about in tight, cohesive flocks, sometimes of up to 200 birds. The unmistakeable feature of these birds is the truly cute head plumage. • These quails typically fall prey to feral cats, but most predatory birds and mammals would make the effort to catch this plump meal. **Where found:** chaparral, brush, suburban parks and oak and riparian woodlands.

# Common Loon

### Gavia immer

**Length:** 28–35 in
**Wingspan:** 4–5 ft

When the haunting call of the common loon
pierces a still evening, cottagers know that summer has begun.
Loons actually have several different calls. A single loon will give a laughing
distress call, separated pairs seem to wail *where aaare you?* and groups give soft,
cohesive hoots as they fly. • Most birds have hollow bones, but loons have solid
bones, which reduces their buoyancy and enables them to dive to maximum
depths of 180 ft. **Where found:** *Breeding:* large lakes and rivers, often with vegetative
islands or even muskrat lodges to nest on. *Winter:* ocean and brackish sounds;
lakes and ponds east of the Cascades.

# Eared Grebe

### Podiceps nigricollis

**Length:** 11½–14 in
**Wingspan:** 16 in

Eared grebes undergo cyclical periods
of atrophy and hypertrophy of their
internal organs and pectoral muscles,
depending on whether or not the birds need to
migrate. This strategy leaves eared grebes flightless for up to 10 months
annually—longer than any other flying bird in the world. • Typically colonial
nesters, these grebes make floating platform nests among thick vegetation on the
edge of a lake or wetland. **Where found:** wetlands, large lakes and sewage disposal
ponds; common summer residents on ponds and marshes east of the Cascades.
**Also known as:** black-necked grebe.

# American White Pelican

### Pelecanus erythrorhynchos

**Length:** 4½–6 ft
**Wingspan:** 9 ft

The American white pelican is one of
only a few bird species that feeds
cooperatively, herding fish into a school and then scooping up its prey in its
bucket-like bill. This impressive feat inspired poet Dixon Lanier Merritt to
write: "A wonderful bird is a pelican. His bill will hold more than his belican!"
• American white pelicans are colonial nesters on low-lying, rocky islands. The
pair incubates only 2 large (3⅜ × 2¼ in) eggs for 29–36 days. **Where found:** lakes,
river mouths and marshes.

# Double-crested Cormorant

### *Phalacrocorax auritus*

**Length:** 26–32 in
**Wingspan:** 4¼ ft

The double-crested cormorant looks like a bird but smells and swims like a fish. With a long, rudder-like tail, excellent underwater vision, sealed nostrils for diving and "wettable" feathers (lacking oil glands), this bird has mastered the underwater world. Cormorants often perch with their wings partially spread to dry their feathers. • They are colonial nesters and build their nests on platforms of sticks and guano. • A traditional Japanese fishing method called *Ukai* employs cormorants on leashes to catch fish. **Where found:** large lakes and large, meandering rivers; nests on islands or in trees.

# Great Blue Heron

### *Ardea herodias*

**Length:** 4¼–4½ ft
**Wingspan:** 6 ft

The long-legged great blue heron has a stealthy, often motionless hunting strategy. It waits for a fish or frog to approach, spears the prey with its bill, then flips its catch into the air and swallows whole. Herons usually hunt near water, but they also stalk fields and meadows in search of rodents. • Great blue herons settle in communal treetop nests called rookeries, and nest width can reach 4 ft. **Where found:** forages along edges of rivers, lakes and marshes; also in fields and meadows.

# Black-crowned Night-Heron

### *Nycticorax nycticorax*

**Length:** 23–26 in
**Wingspan:** 3½ ft

When dusk's long shadows shroud the marshes, black-crowned night-herons arrive to hunt in the marshy waters. These herons crouch motionless, using their large, light-sensitive eyes to spot prey lurking in the shallows. • Watch for them in summer at dawn and dusk as they fly between nesting and feeding areas. The breeding pair builds a nest and incubates 3–4 pale green eggs for 21–26 days. **Where found:** shallow cattail and bulrush marshes; lakeshores and along slow rivers.

# Turkey Vulture

*Cathartes aura*

**Length:** 25–31 in
**Wingspan:** 5½–6 ft

Turkey vultures are playful and social birds, and groups live and sleep together in large trees, or roosts. Some roost sites are over a century old and have been used by the same family of vultures for several generations.
• The genus name *Cathartes* means "cleanser" and refers to this bird's affinity for carrion. • No other bird uses updrafts and thermals in flight as well as the turkey vulture. Pilots have reported seeing vultures soaring at 20,000 ft. **Where found:** usually flies over open country, shorelines or roads; rarely over forests.

# Osprey

*Pandion haliaetus*

**Length:** 22–25 in
**Wingspan:** 5½–6 ft

While hunting for fish, the large and powerful osprey hovers in the air before hurling itself in a dramatic headfirst dive. An instant before striking the water, it rights itself and thrusts its feet forward to grasp its quarry. • Ospreys build bulky nests on high, artificial structures such as communication towers and utility poles, or on buoys and channel markers over water, where the pair tends to 2–3 chicks. **Where found:** lakes and slow-flowing rivers and streams. *In migration:* estuaries and bays.

# Bald Eagle

*Haliaeetus leucocephalus*

**Length:** 30–43 in
**Wingspan:** 5½–8 ft

While soaring hundreds of feet high in the air, bald eagles can spot fish swimming under water and small rodents scurrying through the grass. • Bald eagles do not mature until their fourth or fifth year. Only then do they develop the characteristic white head and tail plumage. • Bald eagles mate for life and renew pair bonds by adding sticks to their same nest each year; the nest can be up to 15 ft in diameter—the largest of any North American bird. **Where found:** around large lakes and rivers.

# Northern Harrier

### *Circus cyaneus*

**Length:** 16–24 in
**Wingspan:** 3½–4 ft

The courtship flight of the northern harrier is a spectacle worth watching in spring. The male climbs almost vertically in the air, then stalls and plummets in a reckless dive toward the ground. At the last second, he saves himself with a hairpin turn that sends him skyward again. • Britain's Royal Air Force named the Harrier aircraft after the northern harrier for its impressive maneuverability. **Where found:** open country; fields, wet meadows, cattail marshes, bogs and croplands; nests on the ground, usually in tall vegetation.

# Sharp-shinned Hawk

### *Accipiter striatus*

**Length:** *Male:* 10–12 in; *Female:* 12–14 in
**Wingspan:** *Male:* 20–24 in; *Female:* 24–28 in

After a successful hunt, the small sharp-shinned hawk often perches on a favorite "plucking post" with its meal in its razor-sharp talons. This *Accipiter*, or woodland hawk, preys almost exclusively on small birds. • Short, rounded wings, a long, rudder-like tail and flap-and-glide flight allow this hawk to maneuver through the forest at high speed. • As it ages, the sharp-shinned hawk's bright yellow eyes become red. **Where found:** dense to semi-open coniferous forests and large woodlots; occasionally along rivers and in urban areas; may visit backyard birdfeeders to prey on feeding sparrows and finches in winter.

# Red-tailed Hawk

### *Buteo jamaicensis*

**Length:** *Male:* 18–23 in; *Female:* 20–25 in
**Wingspan:** 4–5 ft

Spend a summer afternoon in the country, and you will likely see a red-tailed hawk perched on a fence post or soaring on thermals. Courting red-tails will sometimes dive at one another, lock talons and tumble toward the earth, breaking away at the last second to avoid crashing into the ground. • The red-tailed hawk's piercing call is often paired with the image of an eagle in TV commercials and movies. **Where found:** open country with some trees; also roadsides or woodlots; can often be seen flying above cities.

# Rough-legged Hawk

### *Buteo lagopus*

**Length:** 19–24 in
**Wingspan:** 4–4½ ft

When lemming and vole numbers are high in their arctic breeding grounds, these hawks can produce up to 7 young, resulting in many sightings in our area. In lean years, a pair is fortunate to raise a single chick, and sightings here are more rare. • Rough-legged hawks show great variety in coloration, from a whitish light morph to almost entirely dark morphs, both with contrasting patterning. • This *Buteo* often hovers in a stationary position, an adaptation to hunting in open-country habitat that often lacks high perches. **Where found:** fields, wet meadows, open bogs and agricultural croplands.

# American Kestrel

### *Falco sparverius*

**Length:** 7½–8 in
**Wingspan:** 20–24 in

The colorful American kestrel, formerly known as the "sparrow hawk," is a common and widespread bird, not shy of human activity and adaptable to habitat change. This small falcon has benefited from the grassy rights-of-way created by interstate highways; they provide habitat for grasshoppers, which make up most of its diet, as well as other small prey such as mice. **Where found:** along rural roadways, perched on poles and telephone wires; agricultural and open fields, grasslands, riparian woodlands, woodlots, forest edges, bogs, roadside ditches and grassy highway medians.

# Peregrine Falcon

### *Falco peregrinus*

**Length:** *Male:* 15–17 in; *Female:* 17–19 in
**Wingspan:** *Male:* 3–3½ ft; *Female:* 3½–4 ft

Nothing causes more panic in a flock of ducks or shorebirds than a hunting peregrine falcon. This agile raptor matches every twist and turn the flock makes, then dives to strike a lethal blow. • The peregrine falcon is the world's fastest bird. In a headfirst dive, it can reach speeds of up to 220 mph. • Peregrine falcons represent a successful conservation effort since the banning of DDT in North America in 1972. **Where found:** lakeshores, river valleys, river mouths, urban areas and open fields; nests on rocky cliffs or skyscraper ledges.

93

# Sora

### *Porzana carolina*

**Length:** 8–10 in
**Wingspan:** 14 in

The sora has a small body and large, chicken-like feet. Even without webbed feet, this unique creature swims quite well over short distances. • Two rising *or-Ah or-Ah* whistles followed by a strange, descending whinny indicate that a sora is nearby. This secretive bird is hard to spot because it usually remains hidden in dense marshland, but it will occasionally venture into the shallows to search for aquatic insects and mollusks. **Where found:** wetlands with abundant emergent cattails, bulrushes, sedges and grasses.

# Sandhill Crane

### *Grus canadensis*

**Length:** 3¼–4¼ ft
**Wingspan:** 6–7 ft

The sandhill crane's deep, rattling call can be heard long before this bird passes overhead. At first glance, large, V-shaped flocks of sandhill cranes look like flocks of Canada geese, but the cranes often soar and circle in the air, and they do not honk like geese. • Cranes mate for life and reinforce pair bonds each spring with an elaborate courtship dance. **Where found:** *Breeding:* isolated, open marshes, fens and bogs lined with trees or shrubs; nests in the water or along the shoreline on a large mound of aquatic vegetation. *In migration:* agricultural fields and shorelines.

# Black-bellied Plover

### *Pluvialis squatarola*

**Length:** 10½–13 in
**Wingspan:** 29 in

Black-bellied plovers may be seen along the coast during winter months roosting in tight flocks or running along the mudflats when the tide goes out. These large plovers forage for small invertebrates with a robin-like run-and-stop technique, frequently pausing to lift their heads for a reassuring scan of their surroundings. • Watch for small flocks flashing their bold white wing stripes as they fly low over the water's surface. **Where found:** coastal mudflats and beaches; plowed fields, sod farms and meadows; the edges of lakes and reservoirs.

# Snowy Plover

### Charadrius alexandrinus

**Length:** 6–7 in
**Wingspan:** 16–17 in

A year-round occupant of a few relatively undisturbed
coastal beaches, the snowy plover is an endangered
species in our area. Human activity and development are its greatest threats. • The female lays her
eggs on the bare ground, where they are easily trampled; therefore, most nesting
locations are marked off-limits to people. • In the non-breeding season, the snowy
plover is a special bird to see, with the typical run-and-stop foraging along the
waves on the beach. **Where found:** sandy beaches, dunes, sandspits, drier areas of
tidal estuaries and shorelines of alkaline lakes.

# Killdeer

### Charadrius vociferus

**Length:** 9–11 in
**Wingspan:** 24 in

The killdeer is a gifted actor, well known for its
"broken wing" distraction display. When an
intruder wanders too close to its nest (on open
ground in a shallow, usually unlined depres-
sion), the killdeer greets the interloper
with piteous cries while dragging a wing and stumbling about as if injured.
Most predators take the bait and follow, and once the killdeer has lured the
predator far away from its nest, it miraculously recovers from the injury and flies
off with a loud call. **Where found:** open, wet meadows, lakeshores, sandy beaches,
mudflats, gravel streambeds and golf courses.

# Black Oystercatcher

### Haematopus bachmani

**Length:** 17 in
**Wingspan:** 31 in

Black oystercatchers are devoted to their rocky
shoreline habitat, where their meals of limpets, mussels
and snails are abundant. Their flamboyant, red bills are
well adapted for prying open tightly sealed shells. • The
young stay with their parents for up to a year while they
perfect their foraging technique and avoid predators such
as ravens and crows; if they survive the early perils of their
first year, life at the beach can be as long as 15 years! **Where
found:** rocky shorelines and islands; breakwaters, jetties and reefs.

# American Avocet

### *Recurvirostra americana*

**Length:** 17–18 in
**Wingspan:** 31 in

An American avocet in full breeding plumage, with a peachy red head and neck, needle-like bill and black and white body, paints an elegant picture against the uniform mudflats. • Females have been known to parasitize the nests of other avocets and perhaps other species. Conversely, avocets have incubated common tern and black-necked stilt eggs, raising the adopted nestlings along with their own young. **Where found:** *Breeding:* lakeshores, alkaline wetlands and exposed mudflats. *In migration:* reservoirs and lakeshores.

# Spotted Sandpiper

### *Actitis macularius*

**Length:** 7–8 in
**Wingspan:** 15 in

The female spotted sandpiper diligently defends her territory, mates, lays her eggs and leaves the male to tend the clutch. Only about 1% of birds display this unusual breeding strategy known as polyandry. She may mate with several different males, lay up to 4 clutches and produce 20 eggs in a summer. The male then incubates the eggs for 20–24 days, taking on this role because of a relatively high level of prolactin—a hormone known to promote parental care. **Where found:** shorelines, gravel beaches, drainage ditches, swamps and sewage lagoons; occasionally cultivated fields.

# Greater Yellowlegs

### *Tringa melanoleuca*

**Length:** 13–15 in
**Wingspan:** 28 in

The greater yellowlegs and lesser yellowlegs *(T. flavipes)* are medium-sized sandpipers with very similar plumages and very yellow legs and feet. The species differ only subtly, and a solitary greater yellowlegs is difficult to identify until it flushes and utters its distinctive 3 peeps (the lesser yellowlegs peeps twice). As its name suggests, the greater yellowlegs is the larger species and has a slightly upturned, longer bill that is about 1½ times the width of its head. **Where found:** any type of shallow wetland, whether freshwater, brackish or salt; flooded agricultural fields.

# Long-billed Curlew

### Numenius americanus

**Length:** 20–26 in
**Wingspan:** 34–35 in

The long-billed curlew is North America's largest sandpiper, and the downcurved bill of some females may be more than 7 in long. This fine dining utensil can snap up grasshoppers and beetles in long grass as well as reach into the mud and pinch up deeply buried aquatic invertebrates. • The male curlew performs spectacular flight displays over his territory, flying up high while singing out loud, ringing calls and then gliding down in undulating swoops back to the ground. **Where found:** *Breeding:* grasslands interspersed with freshwater lakes and marshes. *In migration:* grasslands, tidal mudflats, estuaries, saltwater marshes and pastures.

# Black Turnstone

### Arenaria melanocephala

**Length:** 9 in
**Wingspan:** 21 in

Turnstones got their name from their foraging technique of turning over stones and other loose objects in search of small crustaceans and mollusks such as barnacles and limpets. • Black turnstones retain a dark plumage year round and are common all along our coastline in winter, but they do not nest here. • They are often seen in small flocks displaying aggressive behavior toward each other and other species. **Where found:** rocky shorelines, breakwaters, jetties and reefs; may visit beaches with seaweed wracks as well as mudflats, gravel bars and temporary ponds.

# Western Sandpiper

### Calidris mauri

**Length:** 6–7 in
**Wingspan:** 14 in

The western sandpiper is a member of a group of sandpipers known as "peeps" in North America and "stints" elsewhere in the English-speaking world. All peeps are similar in plumage, but they are recognized as a group by their exuberant aerial maneuvers: flocks wheel over estuarine tidal flats. • The western sandpiper breeds only in Alaska and extreme northeastern Siberia but passes through our area in large numbers in migration and can be seen on most of our coast in winter. **Where found:** tidal estuaries, saltwater marshes, sandy beaches, freshwater shorelines, flooded fields and pools.

# Dunlin

### *Calidris alpina*

**Length:** 7–9 in
**Wingspan:** 17 in

The dunlin is our most common winter shorebird and can often be seen in very large flocks at tide-line roosts. Its winter plumage is unfortunately rather drab, but by spring, just before it gets ready to migrate, you may start to see its more attractive summer plumage of lovely russet on its back and bold black on its belly. **Where found:** tidal and saltwater marshes, estuaries, lagoon shorelines, open sandy ocean beaches, flooded fields and muddy wetlands; coastal winter resident and migrant through the interior.

# Long-billed Dowitcher

### *Limnodromus scolopaceus*

**Length:** 11–12 in
**Wingspan:** 19 in

The beautiful breeding plumage of this shorebird makes it one of the most anticipated returning migrants to our area. • Long-billed dowitchers favor freshwater habitats, even along the coast, preferring lakeshores, flooded pastures, grass-dotted marshes and the mouths of brackish tidal channels. They nest only along the Beaufort Sea in extreme northern Alaska and northwestern Canada. **Where found:** along lakeshores, shallow marshes and some areas of the coast; common migrant on fresh water.

# Wilson's Snipe

### *Gallinago delicata*

**Length:** 10½–11½ in
**Wingspan:** 18 in

When flushed from cover, snipes perform a series of aerial zigzags to confuse predators. Because of this habit, hunters who were skilled enough to shoot snipes became known as "snipers," a term later adopted by the military. • Courting snipes make an eerie, winnowing sound, like a rapidly hooting owl. The male's specialized outer tail feathers vibrate rapidly in the air as he performs daring, headfirst dives high above a wetland. **Where found:** cattail and bulrush marshes, sedge meadows, poorly drained floodplains, bogs and fens; willow and dogwood tangles.

# Bonaparte's Gull

### *Larus philadelphia*

**Length:** 12–14 in
**Wingspan:** 33 in

This gull's jet-black head in breeding plumage gives it an appealing elegance; its head turns to white in the non-breeding season. • The small, dignified Bonaparte's gull is nothing like its brash relatives. It avoids landfills, preferring to dine on insects caught in the air or plucked from the water's surface. • This gull was named after Charles-Lucien Bonaparte, nephew of Napoleon Bonaparte. He was a naturalist who made significant ornithological contributions in the 1800s. **Where found:** *In migration and winter:* large lakes, rivers and marine nearshore upwellings.

# Ring-billed Gull

### *Larus delawarensis*

**Length:** 18–20 in
**Wingspan:** 4 ft

Few people can claim that they have never seen this common and widespread gull. Highly tolerant of humans, ring-billed gulls will eat almost anything as they swarm parks, beaches, golf courses and fast-food parking lots looking for food handouts and making pests of themselves. However, few species have adjusted to human development as well as the ring-billed gull, which is something to appreciate. • To differentiate between gulls, pay attention to the markings on their bills and the color of their legs and eyes. **Where found:** *Breeding:* rocky, shrubby islands and sewage ponds. *In migration and winter:* lakes, rivers, landfills, golf courses, fields and parks.

# Western Gull

### *Larus occidentalis*

**Length:** 24–26 in
**Wingspan:** 5 ft

This is "the" Pacific Coast seagull—one cannot overlook its conspicuous size and presence. It is a year-round resident on much of our coastline and is a colonial nester on coastal rocks with some vegetative cover. The western gull is not large in numbers, however, with fewer than 200 breeding colonies in total. There is concern that the effects of pesticides on reproduction, threats from oil spills and extensive hybridization with other gulls is compromising its population status. **Where found:** offshore rocks, intertidal and shallow inshore zones, open ocean upwellings, coastal fields and coastal towns.

# Caspian Tern

### *Sterna caspia*

**Length:** 19–23 in
**Wingspan:** 4–4½ ft

The North American Caspian tern population has dramatically increased in the last half-century, mainly because of nesting habitat provided by human-made dredge-spoil islands and dikes. • Adults ferociously defend breeding colonies, aggressively attacking and dive-bombing potential predators, and are extremely sensitive to disturbance—birdwatchers are advised to keep their distance. • Believed to live an average of 12 years, the oldest wild Caspian tern lived more than 26 years! The Caspian tern is the largest tern in the world. **Where found:** beaches, mudflats, sandbars, lakes and flooded agricultural fields.

# Common Murre

### *Uria aalge*

**Length:** 16–17 in
**Wingspan:** 26 in

Common murres spend much of their lives at sea and only come ashore to breed, nesting in huge, tightly packed colonies of up to tens of thousands of birds. • Pelagic boat tours are a fantastic way to see common murres in action. These skilled swimmers use their small wings, webbed feet and sleek, waterproof plumage to pursue fish underwater. Murres can remain beneath the surface for more than a minute and regularly dive to depths of 100 ft. **Where found:** *Breeding:* offshore islands, islets and rocks. *Foraging:* open ocean from just beyond the surf zone to miles offshore.

# Marbled Murrelet

### *Brachyramphus marmoratus*

**Length:** 9–10 in
**Wingspan:** 16 in

Marbled murrelets are one of the most unusual seabirds on the Pacific coast. These secretive birds nest deep within the mossy heights of old-growth forests but return to the ocean to feed. Each night for a month, adults bring their single, hungry nestling fish from the sea, sometimes flying 40 mi each way. Marbled murrelets' dependence on old-growth forests and coastal habitats often conflicts with human interests. **Where found:** along ocean shoreline and around harbor entrances; favor sandy bottoms opposite rocky shores. *Breeding:* dense, coniferous forests, particularly stands of old-growth coast Douglas-fir and sitka spruce.

# Tufted Puffin

### *Fratercula cirrhata*

**Length:** 15–16 in
**Wingspan:** 25 in

Famous for their flamboyant bills and cavalier head tufts, tufted puffins are an added attraction on West Coast whale-watching tours. • A puffin can line up more than 12 small fish crosswise in its bill, using its round tongue and serrated upper mandible to keep the hoard in place. • Stubby wings propel alcids with surprising speed and agility underwater, but these features make for awkward takeoffs and laborious flight. **Where found:** *Breeding:* offshore islands with soil burrows; upwellings near islands. *Winter:* deep, offshore ocean.

# Rock Pigeon

### *Columba livia*

**Length:** 12–13 in
**Wingspan:** 28 in; male is usually larger

This pigeon is likely a descendant of a Eurasian bird that was first domesticated about 4500 BC. Both Caesar and Napoleon used rock pigeons as message couriers. European settlers introduced the rock pigeon to North America in the 17th century, and today, it is familiar to most anyone who has lived in a city. • No other "wild" bird varies as much in coloration, a result of semi-domestication and extensive inbreeding over time. **Where found:** urban areas, railway yards and agricultural areas; high cliffs often provide more natural habitat. **Also known as:** rock dove.

# Mourning Dove

### *Zenaida macroura*

**Length:** 11–13 in
**Wingspan:** 18 in

The mourning dove's soft cooing, which filters through broken woodlands and suburban parks, is often confused with the sound of a hooting owl. • This dove is one of the most abundant native birds in North America, with increased numbers and range since human development created more open habitats and food sources, such as waste grain and birdfeeders. • Mourning doves lay only 2 eggs at a time, but up to 6 broods each year—more than any other native bird. **Where found:** open and riparian woodlands, forest edges, agricultural and suburban areas and open parks.

# Western Screech-Owl

### *Megascops kennicottii*

**Length:** *Male:* 8–9 in; *Female:* 10–11 in
**Wingspan:** *Male:* 18–20 in; *Female:* 22–24 in

The western screech-owl is a fierce and adaptable nocturnal hunter, often adding birds larger than itself to its usual diet of insects, amphibians and small mammals. • This chunky, open-woodland owl requires little more than a secluded roosting site in dense shrubs or a tree hollow (also in which to nest) over semi-open ground that it can scout from low tree limbs. **Where found:** mid-elevation forests including coniferous forests with juniper stands; chaparral and oak woodlands and riparian woodlands; towns, orchards, farms, ranches and desert oases.

# Great Horned Owl

### *Bubo virginianus*

**Length:** 18–25 in
**Wingspan:** 3–5 ft

This highly adaptable and superbly camouflaged hunter has sharp hearing and powerful vision that allow it to hunt by night and day. It will swoop down from a perch onto almost any small creature that moves. • The leading edge of the flight feathers is fringed rather than smooth, which interrupts airflow over the wing and allows the owl to fly noiselessly. • The great horned owl has a poor sense of smell, which might explain why it is the only consistent predator of skunks. **Where found:** fragmented forests, fields, riparian woodlands, suburban parks and wooded edges of landfills.

# Burrowing Owl

### *Athene cunicularia*

**Length:** 9–11 in
**Wingspan:** 21–24 in

The burrowing owl is a loyal inhabitant of the prairie grasslands. During the day, this owl perches on top of fence posts or at the entrance to its burrow, where it looks very similar to a ground squirrel, in whose abandoned burrows it nests. • The extermination of ground squirrels in the prairies has greatly reduced the number of suitable nest sites for the endangered burrowing owl, which is also threatened by collisions with vehicles, the effect of agricultural chemicals and the conversion of native grasslands to croplands. **Where found:** open, short-grass hayfields, pastures and prairies; occasionally lawns and golf courses.

# Spotted Owl

### *Strix occidentalis*

**Length:** 17–19 in
**Wingspan:** 3½ ft

The spotted owl unwittingly became the center of public attention in the Pacific Northwest when protecting this endangered species threatened to halt logging in coastal old-growth forests that this owl and many other species require to survive. The spotted owl has become a symbol for preserving this unique habitat and a reminder to balance the value of nature with our economic values. Spotted owl habitat is often dominated by Douglas-fir because the owl's main prey, flying squirrels, feed on a fungus that grows on fir trees. **Where found:** old-growth coniferous and mixed conifer-hardwood forest; wanderers or dispersing juveniles are occasionally well outside typical habitat.

# Common Nighthawk

### *Chordeiles minor*

**Length:** 8–10 in
**Wingspan:** 23–26 in

In an energetic courting display, the male common nighthawk dives and then swerves skyward, making a hollow booming sound with its wings. • The common nighthawk, as with all nightjars, has adapted to catch insects in midair: its large, gaping mouth is surrounded by feather shafts that funnel insects into its bill. It can eat over 2600 insects in one day, including mosquitoes, blackflies and flying ants. **Where found:** *Breeding:* forest openings, bogs, rocky outcroppings and gravel rooftops. *In migration:* often near water; any area with large numbers of flying insects.

# Vaux's Swift

### *Chaetura vauxi*

**Length:** 5 in
**Wingspan:** 12 in

Swifts arrive in spring and quickly and collectively plunge into chimneys and other cavities to roost. They build their nests in cavities by pasting loosely woven twigs together with their sticky saliva. • Rather than perching like most birds, swifts use their small, strong claws to grab onto vertical surfaces. They feed on the wing, hawking for flying ants, moths and other insects. **Where found:** *Breeding:* mixed and coniferous old-growth forests, particularly of grand fir. *In migration:* towns and their chimneys.

# Anna's Hummingbird

### *Calypte anna*

**Length:** 3–4 in
**Wingspan:** 5–5½ in

Once restricted as a nesting species to the Pacific slope of northern Baja California and Southern California, Anna's hummingbird expanded its range northward along the coast after the 1930s, and today, we get to enjoy this beautiful hummer. • Hummingbirds are easily lured to our gardens with exotic, nectar-producing plants and/or hummingbird feeders. **Where found:** riparian areas, coastal scrubland, farmlands and urban gardens; fairly common year-round resident of the Puget Trough and southern sites along the coast and present in winter in surrounding areas.

# Rufous Hummingbird

### *Selasphorus rufus*

**Length:** 3–3½ in
**Wingspan:** 4½ in

Rufous hummingbirds are tiny, delicate
avian jewels, but their beauty hides
a relentless mean streak; these birds
buzz past one another at nectar sites and
chase rivals for some distances. • Hummingbirds beat their
wings up to 80 times per second, their hearts can beat up to 1200 times per
minute, and they are capable of flying at speeds up to 60 mph. **Where found:**
nearly any habitat with abundant flowers, including gardens; edges of coniferous
and deciduous forests; burned sites; brushy slopes and alpine meadows.

# Belted Kingfisher

### *Ceryle alcyon*

**Length:** 11–14 in
**Wingspan:** 20–21 in

Perched on a bare branch over a productive
pool, the "king of the fishers" plunges headfirst into the water, snatches up a fish or a frog,
flips it into the air then swallows it headfirst.
Nestlings are able to swallow small fish
whole at only 5 days old. • In Greek
mythology, Alcyon, the daughter of the wind god, grieved so deeply for her
drowned husband that the gods transformed them both into kingfishers. **Where
found:** rivers, large streams, lakes, marshes and beaver ponds, especially near
exposed soil banks, gravel pits or bluffs.

# Lewis's Woodpecker

### *Melanerpes lewis*

**Length:** 11 in
**Wingspan:** 21 in

Rejecting the traditional life of a woodpecker, Lewis's woodpecker chooses to forage away from the tree and instead
catch insects on the wing. It will often perch on wires or in
semi-open countryside atop a pole or snag and observe the
world beyond the forest. • Competition with European
starlings for nesting holes has threatened this woodpecker's
numbers; it is now a candidate for state threatened lists.
**Where found:** eastern Cascade slopes; open woodlands,
Garry oak woodlands and riparian ponderosa pines
and cottonwoods.

# Downy Woodpecker

### *Picoides pubescens*

**Length:** 6–7 in
**Wingspan:** 12 in

A birdfeeder well stocked with peanut butter and black-oil sunflower seeds may attract a pair of downy woodpeckers to your backyard. These approachable little birds are more tolerant of human activity than most other species, and they visit feeders more often than the larger, more aggressive hairy woodpeckers (*P. villosus*). • Downy woodpeckers' white outer tail feathers have several dark spots, while the hairy woodpeckers' are pure white. **Where found:** any wooded environment, especially deciduous and mixed forests and areas with tall, deciduous shrubs.

# Northern Flicker

### *Colaptes auratus*

**Length:** 12–13 in
**Wingspan:** 20 in

The northern flicker scours the ground and tree trunks in search of invertebrates, particularly ants that it squashes and preens itself with for the formic acid, which kills small parasites on its skin and feathers. • There are 2 races of northern flicker: the yellow-shafted flicker of eastern North America has yellow underwings and undertail coverts; the red-shafted flicker of the West has reddish underwings and undertail coverts. The red-shafted race is the widespread breeder in our area, but some yellow-shafts appear as migrants and winter residents. **Where found:** *Breeding:* open woodlands and forest edges, fields, meadows, beaver ponds and other wetlands. *In migration and winter:* coastal vegetation, offshore islands and urban gardens.

# Olive-sided Flycatcher

### *Contopus cooperi*

**Length:** 7–8 in
**Wingspan:** 13 in

The olive-sided flycatcher's upright, attentive posture contrasts with its comical song: *quick-three-beers! quick-three-beers!* As a dutiful parent, this flycatcher changes its tune during nesting, when it more often produces an equally enthusiastic *pip-pip-pip*. It builds its nest of twigs bound with spider silk high in a conifer, usually on a branch far from the trunk. • This bird's numbers are declining, and it is a federal species of concern. **Where found:** semi-open mixed and coniferous forests near water; prefers burned areas and wetlands.

# Western Wood-Pewee

### *Contopus sordidulus*

**Length:** 5–6 in
**Wingspan:** 10½ in

Aspiring birders will quickly come to recognize the burry,
down-slurred call of the western wood-pewee as one of the
most common summertime noises. • The nest is a model
of concealment, looking like little more than a bump on
a limb; but, if it is discovered by predators, this flycatcher will aggressively defend it. • Overall numbers
of western wood-pewees appear to be declining, potentially because of loss or alteration of habitat through
clear-cutting or grazing. **Where found:** most semi-open forest habitats including
cottonwood riparian, ponderosa pine and montane coniferous or mixed woodlands, orchards and residential woodlots.

# Pacific-slope Flycatcher

### *Empidonax difficilis*

**Length:** 5 in
**Wingspan:** 8 in

Flycatchers are hard to distinguish from each other, and it
was not until late in the 20th century that the Pacific-slope
flycatcher was recognized as its own species. Nevertheless,
it is a common songbird in our area, and its song is
more distinctive than its looks. The upslurred *suweeet*
call is a familiar sound in any moist woodland in
spring. • This flycatcher sits perched on exposed
branches, stalking its insect prey that it swoops down on to catch, or "hawk,"
in flight. **Where found:** moist hardwood or mixed forests in foothills and valleys.

# Western Kingbird

### *Tyrannus verticalis*

**Length:** 8–9 in
**Wingspan:** 15½ in

Kingbirds are a group of flycatchers that perch on wires or
fence posts in open habitats and fearlessly chase out larger
birds from their breeding territories. • In tumbling aerial
courtship displays, the male flies to heights of 65 ft above
the ground, stalls, then tumbles and flips his way back to
the earth. **Where found:** *Breeding:* irrigated valleys, open
or riparian woodlands and woodland edges. *In migration
and winter:* any fairly open habitat.

# Northern Shrike

## *Lanius excubitor*

**Length:** 10 in
**Wingspan:** 14–15 in

One of the most vicious predators in the bird world, the northern shrike relies on its sharp, hooked bill to catch and kill small birds or rodents, which it spots from treetop perches. Its tendency to impale its prey on thorns and barbs for later consumption has earned it the name "butcher bird." • Shrikes are the world's only true carnivorous songbirds. • Northern shrikes visit our region each winter in unpredictable and highly variable numbers. **Where found:** semi-open country, scrub, low-elevation orchards, farmlands and ranches; migrants often appear among dunes or in coastal scrub.

# Warbling Vireo

## *Vireo gilvus*

**Length:** 5–5½ in
**Wingspan:** 8–9 in

The charming warbling vireo is a common spring and summer resident, often settling close to urban areas; its velvety voice has a warbling quality not heard in other vireos and is more distinctive than its looks—it lacks any splashy field marks. • It nests in a horizontal fork of a tree or shrub, making a hanging basket-like cup nest of grass, roots, plant down and spider silk. **Where found:** *Breeding:* riparian wooded areas, open bigleaf maple forests and mixed forests. *In migration:* almost any woodlands; prefers hardwood stands and residential areas.

# Steller's Jay

## *Cyanocitta stelleri*

**Length:** 11–12 in
**Wingspan:** 19 in

With a dark crest and velvet blue feathers, the stunning Steller's jay is a resident jewel in our forests. Generally noisy and pugnacious, this bird suddenly becomes silent and cleverly elusive when nesting. • Bold Steller's jays will not hesitate to steal food scraps from inattentive picnickers and scatter smaller birds at feeders. Their ability to adapt, learn and even take advantage of situations shows the intelligence of corvids. **Where found:** coniferous and mixed woodlands; coastal and mountain conifers to the timberline.

# Clark's Nutcracker

### *Nucifraga columbiana*

**Length:** 12–13 in
**Wingspan:** 24 in

Clark's nutcracker has a long, sturdy bill for prying apart the cones of conifers and a special throat pouch for transporting the seeds to carefully selected storage spots. These caches might be 8 mi or more apart, and together may contain more than 30,000 seeds. Over winter and throughout the nesting cycle, nutcrackers use their phenomenal memory to relocate cache sites. Pines rely on Clark's nutcracker for seed dispersal. **Where found:** upper-elevation conifer forests; campgrounds and picnic areas.

# Black-billed Magpie

### *Pica hudsonia*

**Length:** 18 in
**Wingspan:** 25 in

Truly among North America's most beautiful birds, black-billed magpies are also exceptional architects, building elaborate, domed, stick and twig nests held together with mud. They are famed interior designers as well, picking up any shiny objects they can carry to decorate their nests with. These prized homes have high re-sell value, remaining in trees for years and being used by other birds. • Albino magpies occasionally occur, with white bellies and light gray, instead of black, body feathers. **Where found:** open forests, agricultural areas, riparian thickets, townsites and campgrounds.

# American Crow

### *Corvus brachyrhynchos*

**Length:** 17–21 in
**Wingspan:** 36 in

The noise that most often emanates from these treetop squawkers seems unrepresentative of their intelligence. Crows will often drop walnuts or clams from great heights onto a hard surface to crack the shells. These wary, clever birds are also impressive mimics, able to whine like a dog and laugh or cry like a human. • Crows are family oriented, and the young from the previous year may help their parents raise the nestlings. **Where found:** urban areas, agricultural fields and other open areas with scattered woodlands.

# Common Raven

### *Corvus corax*

**Length:** 21–23 in
**Wingspan:** 4 ft

The common raven soars with a wingspan comparable to that of hawk, traveling along coastlines, over deserts, along mountain ridges and even over the arctic tundra. Few birds occupy such a large natural range. • From producing complex vocalizations to playfully sliding down snow banks, this raucous bird exhibits behaviors that many people once thought of as exclusively human. Glorified in Native American culture, the raven seems to demonstrate an apparent enjoyment of life. **Where found:** coniferous and mixed forests and woodlands; townsites, campgrounds and landfills.

# Horned Lark

### *Eremophila alpestris*

**Length:** 7 in
**Wingspan:** 12 in

One way to distinguish a sparrow from a horned lark is by its method of locomotion: horned larks walk, but sparrows hop. • This bird's dark tail contrasts with its light brown body and belly, and it has 2 unique black "horns." Look for this feature to spot the horned lark in its open-country habitat. • In spring, the male performs an impressive, high-speed, plummeting courtship dive. **Where found:** bare alpine sites and short-grass habitats; deserts, farmlands and roadsides. *Winter*: agricultural fields and beaches.

# Violet-green Swallow

### *Tachycineta thalassina*

**Length:** 5–5½ in
**Wingspan:** 13½ in

Their affinity for cliffs, open areas, natural tree cavities and nest boxes allows violet-green swallows to inhabit diverse habitats. • Swallows are swift and graceful fliers, routinely traveling at speeds of 30 mph. They catch flying insects such as flies, flying ants and wasps, often foraging at 1000–2000 ft—far higher than other swallows—and drink on the wing by skimming the water's surface. **Where found:** wide variety of open areas near water including open woodlands, wooded canyons, agricultural lands and towns.

# Black-capped Chickadee

**Poecile atricapillus**

**Length:** 5–6 in
**Wingspan:** 8 in

You can catch a glimpse of these incredibly sociable chickadees at any time of year. While observing their antics at feeders, you may even be able to entice a black-capped chickadee to the palm of your hand with the help of a sunflower seed. • They call out their name with a distinctive *chick-a-dee-dee-dee*, but they also sing a slow, whistled *swee-tee* or *fee-bee*. • Another common chickadee in our area is the chestnut-backed chickadee (*P. rufescens*). It is distinctly more rufous colored. **Where found:** deciduous and mixed forests, riparian woodlands, wooded urban parks and backyard feeders.

# Bushtit

**Psaltriparus minimus**

**Length:** 4–4½ in
**Wingspan:** 6 in

Bushtits catch your eye as they endlessly bounce from one shrubby perch to another and catch your ear with charming, bell-like, tinkling calls. Hyperactive in everything they do, these tiny, fluffy, gregarious birds are constantly on the move, either fastidiously building a nest or roaming about in post-breeding bands of up to 40 members. When nest building, they neurotically test every fiber to ensure its suitability. Bushtits will desert both nest and mate if intruded upon. **Where found:** juniper and oak forests, riparian brushlands and large residential gardens.

# Red-breasted Nuthatch

**Sitta canadensis**

**Length:** 4–4½ in
**Wingspan:** 8 in

The red-breasted nuthatch has a somewhat dizzying view of the world as it moves down tree trunks headfirst, cleaning up the seeds, insects and nuts that woodpeckers may have overlooked. It is also attracted to backyard birdfeeders filled with suet or peanut butter. • This nuthatch excavates a cavity nest or uses an abandoned woodpecker nest and smears the entrance with sap to keep away ants and other insects that can transmit fungal infections or parasitize nestlings. **Where found:** open woodlands, preferring oak and pine on the eastern Cascades.

111

# House Wren

### *Troglodytes aedon*

**Length:** 4½–5 in
**Wingspan:** 6 in

The bland, nondescript plumage of this suburban and city park dweller can go unnoticed until you hear it sing a seemingly unending song. • Like all wrens, the house wren usually carries its short tail raised upward. • A house wren often builds numerous nests, which later serve as decoy nests to fool would-be enemies. This wren can be very aggressive toward other species that nest in its territory, puncturing and tossing eggs from other birds' nests. **Where found:** thickets and shrubby openings in or at the edge of deciduous or mixed woodlands; shrubs and thickets near buildings; mainly in eastern Washington and Oregon.

# Winter Wren

### *Troglodytes troglodytes*

**Length:** 4 in
**Wingspan:** 5½ in

The upraised, mottled brown tail of the winter wren blends well with its habitat of gnarled, upturned roots and decomposing tree trunks. • This tiny bird has a great vocal magnitude—it boldly lays claim to its territory with its call and distinctive, melodious song. The winter wren can sustain its song for 10 seconds, using up to 113 tones. • Although the male winter wren contributes to raising the family by defending the nest and finding food for the nestlings, he sleeps elsewhere at night, in an unfinished nest. **Where found:** lowland forests, woodlands and thickets, preferring wet forests. **Also known as:** Jenny wren.

# American Dipper

### *Cinclus mexicanus*

**Length:** 7½ in; male slightly larger than female
**Wingspan:** 11 in

When you come across a small, dark bird standing on an exposed boulder next to a fast-flowing mountain stream, you have no doubt found an American dipper. This unique, aquatic songbird bends its legs incessantly, bobbing to the roar of the torrent, then suddenly dives into the water. It uses its wings to swim in search of aquatic insect larvae. **Where found:** fast-flowing, rocky streams and rivers with cascades, riffles and waterfalls.

# Golden-crowned Kinglet

### *Regulus satrapa*

**Length:** 4 in
**Wingspan:** 7 in

The dainty golden-crowned kinglet is not much
bigger than a hummingbird, and when it searches for
insects, berries and sap in the forest canopy, it is prone to
unique hazards such as perishing on the burrs of burdock
plants. • "Pishing" and squeaking sounds might lure these songbirds into an
observable range; perpetual motion and chronic wing flicking can help identify
golden-crowns from a distance. **Where found:** *Breeding:* mature coniferous forests
at the tops of spruces, pines and firs. *In migration* and *winter:* coastal forests,
riparian areas and desert oases; sometimes urban parks and gardens.

# American Robin

### *Turdus migratorius*

**Length:** 10 in
**Wingspan:** 17 in

The American robin is a familiar
and common sight on lawns as it
searches for worms. In winter, its
diet switches to fruit trees, which can
attract flocks to feed. • American robins build cup-shaped nests of grass, moss
and mud. The female incubates 4 light blue eggs and raises up to 3 broods per year.
The male cares for the fledglings from the first brood while the female incubates
the second clutch of eggs. **Where found:** *Breeding:* residential lawns and gardens,
pastures, urban parks, broken forests, bogs and river shorelines. *Winter:* near
fruit-bearing trees and springs.

# Wrentit

### *Chamaea fasciata*

**Length:** 6–6½ in
**Wingspan:** 7 in

Unlike most songbirds, wrentits do not migrate, and they
mate for life. They are secretive birds, preferring to remain
concealed within dense tangles of brush and scrub, and they
rarely cross open areas where predators could interrupt
their feeble flights without warning. A pair of wrentits may spend an entire
lifetime together in an area no larger than a few acres. **Where found:** hilly brushland
including lowland and montane chaparral, coastal scrub, sagebrush and shrubby
riparian tangles; readily colonizes regenerating logged sites.

# European Starling

### *Sturnus vulgaris*

**Length:** 8½ in
**Wingspan:** 16 in

The European starling did not hesitate to make itself known across North America after being released in New York City's Central Park in 1890 and 1891. Starlings were brought to New York as part of the local Shakespeare society's plan to introduce all the birds mentioned in their favorite author's writings. • This highly adaptable bird not only took over the nest sites of native cavity nesters, such as woodpeckers, but it also learned to mimic the sounds of killdeers, red-tailed hawks, soras and meadowlarks. **Where found:** *Breeding:* cities, towns, residential areas, farmyards and woodland fringes and clearings. *Winter:* near feedlots and pastures.

# Cedar Waxwing

### *Bombycilla cedrorum*

**Length:** 7 in
**Wingspan:** 12 in

With its black "mask" and slick hairdo, the cedar waxwing has a heroic look. To court a mate, the gentlemanly male hops toward a female and offers her a berry. The female accepts the berry and hops away, then stops and hops back toward the male to offer him the berry in return. **Where found:** *Breeding:* hardwood and mixed forests, woodland edges, fruit orchards, young pine plantations and riparian hardwoods among conifers. *In migration* and *winter:* open woodlands and brush, residential areas and any habitat with nearby berries; often near water.

# Orange-crowned Warbler

### *Vermivora celata*

**Length:** 5 in
**Wingspan:** 7 in

The nondescript orange-crowned warbler causes identification problems for many birders. Its drab, olive yellow appearance and lack of field marks make it frustratingly similar to females of other warbler species, and the male's orange crown patch is seldom visible. • This small warbler is usually seen gleaning insects from the leaves and buds of low shrubs and routinely feeds on sap or insects attracted to the sap wells drilled by other birds. **Where found:** any wooded habitat; areas with tall shrubs.

# Yellow-rumped Warbler

### Dendroica coronata

**Length:** 5½ in
**Wingspan:** 9–9½ in

Yellow-rumped warblers are the most abundant and widespread wood-warblers in North America. Trees laden with fruit attract these birds in winter. • This species comes in 2 forms: the yellow-throated "Audubon's warbler" of the West, and the white-throated "myrtle warbler," which breeds in the North and east of the Rockies. Myrtle warblers do not breed in our area, but they are commonly seen in winter and during migration down the Pacific Coast. **Where found:** *Breeding:* coniferous or mixed forests. *In migration* and *winter:* hardwood and mixed thickets and woodlands along the coast and in interior valleys.

# Black-throated Gray Warbler

### Dendroica nigrescens

**Length:** 5 in
**Wingspan:** 8 in

Only the hint of one spot of yellow appears on the face of this otherwise black-and-white-and-gray warbler, making it easily recognizable; a *weezy-weezy-weezy-wee-zee* song confirms its identity. • This warbler actively searches for insects among the branches of trees and bushes, preferring oaks and junipers. **Where found:** hardwood and mixed forests, second-growth clear-cuts and juniper woodlands; spring and summer resident of the Cascades. *In migration:* towns and riparian areas.

# Townsend's Warbler

### Dendroica townsendi

**Length:** 5 in
**Wingspan:** 8 in

Choosing to nest at the tops of conifer trees in mountain forests, this warbler may be hard to spot outside of winter, when it can be seen with other hardy winter birds in the dense foliage along the coast or in residential gardens with suet feeders. • With an omnivorous appetite, Townsend's warbler gleans vegetation and eats seeds and plant galls but also hawks for insects. **Where found:** *Breeding:* mountain fir and other coniferous forests. *In migration* and *winter:* coniferous and mixed woods, urban parks and coastal thickets.

# Wilson's Warbler

### *Wilsonia pusilla*

**Length:** 4½–5 in
**Wingspan:** 7 in

The petite Wilson's warbler darts energetically through the undergrowth in its tireless search for insects. Fueled by its energy-rich prey, this indefatigable bird seems to behave as if a motionless moment would break some unwritten law of warblerdom. • This bird is named for ornithologist Alexander Wilson, who pioneered studies of North American birds. **Where found:** shrubby riparian habitat; wet mountain meadows and edges of small lakes and springs. *Breeding:* cool, moist riparian habitat with dense, deciduous shrub cover, especially willow and alder.

# Western Tanager

### *Piranga ludoviciana*

**Length:** 7 in
**Wingspan:** 11–11½ in

The western tanager brings with it the colors of a tropical visitor on its summer vacation in our area. This bird raises a new generation of young and takes advantage of the seasonal explosion of food in our forests before heading back to its exotic wintering grounds in Mexico and Central America. • The male western tanager spends long periods of time singing from the same perch, sounding like a robin with a sore throat. **Where found:** mature coniferous and mixed forests, especially ponderosa pine. *In migration:* fruit-bearing trees and shrubs in riparian woodlands.

# Spotted Towhee

### *Pipilo maculatus*

**Length:** 7–8 in
**Wingspan:** 10–10½ in

Spotted towhees are capable of quite a ruckus when they forage in loose leaf litter, scraping with both feet. • Although they are confident birds, not hesitant to scold the family cat, spotted towhees can be shy. They need some coaxing if you want to lure them into the open, and they tend to make themselves scarce in a crowded park. **Where found:** brushy hedgerows and woods with a dense understory; overgrown bushy fields and hillsides; frequently at feeders, especially in winter; tangled thickets and overgrown gardens with blackberries and other small fruits.

# Chipping Sparrow

### Spizella passerina

**Length:** 5–6 in
**Wingspan:** 8½ in

Although you may spot the relatively tame chipping sparrow singing from a high perch, it commonly nests at eye level, so you can easily watch its breeding and nest-building rituals. • This bird's song is very similar to that of the dark-eyed junco but slightly faster, drier and with a less musical series of notes. **Where found:** *Breeding:* grassy woodlands and clearings in dry forests. *In migration* and *winter:* open grasslands with brushy cover, sagebrush scrub and residential woodlots; backyard feeders and lawns.

# Song Sparrow

### Melospiza melodia

**Length:** 6–7 in
**Wingspan:** 8 in

Although its plumage is unremarkable, the well-named song sparrow is among the great singers of the bird world. When a male song sparrow is only a few months old, he has already created a courtship tune of his own, having learned the basics of melody and rhythm from his father and rival males. A well-stocked backyard feeder may be a fair trade for a sweet song in the dead of winter. **Where found:** hardwood brush in forests and open country; near water or in lush vegetation in chaparral, riparian willows, marshy habitats and residential areas.

# White-crowned Sparrow

### Zonotrichia leucophrys

**Length:** 5½–7 in
**Wingspan:** 9½ in

In winter, large, bold and smartly patterned white-crowned sparrows brighten brushy hedgerows, overgrown fields and riparian areas. During cold weather, these sparrows may visit birdfeeders stocked with cracked corn. • Several different races of the white-crowned sparrow occur in North America, all with similar plumage but different song dialects. Research into this sparrow has given science tremendous insight into bird physiology, homing behavior and the geographic variability of song dialects. **Where found:** *Breeding:* coastal and mountain thickets. *In migration:* brushy areas; sometimes residential areas.

# Dark-eyed Junco

### *Junco hyemalis*

**Length:** 6–7 in
**Wingspan:** 9 in

Juncos usually congregate in backyards with birdfeeders and sheltering conifers—with such amenities at their disposal, more and more juncos are appearing in urban areas. These birds spend most of their time on the ground, snatching up seeds underneath birdfeeders, and they are readily flushed from wooded trails. • There are 5 closely related dark-eyed junco subspecies in North America that share similar habits but differ in coloration and range. One of the most common in our area is the Oregon junco (*J. h. oreganus*). **Where found:** shrubby woodland borders and backyard feeders.

# Black-headed Grosbeak

### *Pheucticus melanocephalus*

**Length:** 7–8½ in
**Wingspan:** 12½ in

Black-headed grosbeaks will quickly make your acquaintance on almost any spring or summer hike in the woods. These birds are marvelous singers, advertising breeding territories with extended bouts of complex, accented caroling. Males sing from slightly sheltered perches near the top of a tree, while females forage and conduct nesting chores within the cover of interior foliage. **Where found:** hardwood and mixed forests; bottomland willows and cottonwoods, riparian and lakeshore woodlands, rich oak woodlands and high-elevation aspen groves.

# Red-winged Blackbird

### *Agelaius phoeniceus*

**Length:** 7½–9 in
**Wingspan:** 13 in

The male red-winged blackbird wears his bright red shoulders like armor—together with his short, raspy song, they are key in defending his territory from rivals. • Nearly every cattail marsh worthy of note in our region hosts red-winged blackbirds and resonates with that proud and distinctive song. The female's cryptic coloration allows her to sit inconspicuously on her nest, blending in perfectly among the cattails or shoreline bushes. **Where found:** cattail marshes, wet meadows and ditches, croplands and shoreline shrubs.

# Western Meadowlark

### *Sturnella neglecta*

**Length:** 9–9½ in
**Wingspan:** 14½ in

In the early 19th century, members of the Lewis and Clark expedition overlooked the western meadowlark, mistaking it for the very similar-looking eastern meadowlark, hence the scientific name *neglecta*. • A breeding pair bond is established with an elaborate courtship dance: the male and female face each other, raise their bills high in the air and perform a grassland ballet. • Western meadowlarks have benefited from land management protecting grasslands from overgrazing or agriculture. **Where found:** grassy meadows, native prairie and pastures; also in some croplands, weedy fields and grassy roadsides.

# House Finch

### *Carpodacus mexicanus*

**Length:** 5–6 in
**Wingspan:** 9½ in

Formerly restricted to the arid Southwest and Mexico, the house finch is now commonly found throughout the continental U.S. and has even been introduced to Hawaii. Only the resourceful house finch has been aggressive and stubborn enough to successfully outcompete the house sparrow. • The male house finch's plumage varies in color from light yellow to bright red, but females will choose to breed with the reddest males. **Where found:** disturbed areas, including farms, ranches and towns; open fields and woodlands. *Winter:* backyard feeders.

# Pine Siskin

### *Carduelis pinus*

**Length:** 4½–5½ in
**Wingspan:** 9 in

Pine siskins are unpredictable, social birds that may be abundant for a time, then suddenly disappear. Because their favored habitats are widely scattered, flocks are constantly on the move, searching forests for the most lucrative seed crops. • These drab, sparrow-like birds are easy to overlook at first, but once you recognize their characteristic rising *zzzreeeee* calls and boisterous chatter, you will encounter them with surprising frequency. **Where found:** coniferous forests, though not pines as its name suggests; backyard finch feeders with black niger seed.

# American Goldfinch

### Carduelis tristis

**Length:** 4½–5 in
**Wingspan:** 9 in

Like vibrant rays of sunshine, American goldfinches cheerily flutter over weedy fields, gardens and along roadsides, perching on late-summer thistle heads or poking through dandelion patches in search of seeds. It is hard to miss their jubilant *po-ta-to-chip* call and distinctive, undulating flight style. • Because these acrobatic birds regularly feed while hanging upside down, finch feeders are designed with the seed-openings below the perches. • This bird was adopted as the official state bird of Washington in 1951. **Where found:** weedy fields, woodland edges, meadows, riparian areas, parks and gardens. **Also known as:** willow goldfinch.

# House Sparrow

### Passer domesticus

**Length:** 5½–6½ in
**Wingspan:** 9½ in

This abundant and conspicuous bird was introduced to North America in the 1850s as part of a plan to control the insects that were damaging grain and cereal crops. As it turns out, these birds are largely vegetarian! • The house sparrow will usurp territory and nests of native birds, such as a bluebirds, cliff swallows or purple martins, and has a high reproductive output of 4 clutches per year, with up to 8 young per clutch. **Where found:** townsites, urban and suburban areas, farmyards and agricultural areas, railway yards and other developed areas.

# AMPHIBIANS & REPTILES

Amphibians and reptiles are commonly referred to as cold-blooded, but this is misleading. Although amphibians and reptiles lack the ability to generate their internal body heat, they are not necessarily cold-blooded. These animals are ectothermic or poikilothermic, meaning that the temperature of the surrounding environment governs their body temperature. The animal will obtain heat from sunlight, warm rocks and logs, and warmed earth. Amphibians and reptiles hibernate in winter in cold regions, and some species of reptiles estivate in summer in hot regions. Both amphibians and reptiles moult (shed their skins) as they grow to larger body sizes.

Amphibians are smooth-skinned and most live in moist habitats. They are represented by the salamanders, frogs and toads. They typically lay shell-less eggs in jelly-like masses in water. These eggs hatch into gilled larvae (larvae of frogs and toads are called tadpoles), which then metamorphose into adults with lungs and legs. Amphibians can regenerate their skin and often even entire limbs. Male and female amphibians often differ in size and color, and males may have other diagnostics when sexually mature, such as the vocal sacs in many frogs and toads.

Reptiles are fully terrestrial vertebrates with scaly skin. In this guide, the representatives are turtles, lizards and snakes. Most reptiles lay eggs buried in loose soil, but some snakes and lizards give birth to live young. Reptiles do not have a larval stage.

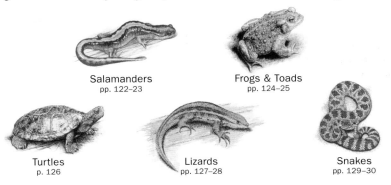

Salamanders
pp. 122–23

Frogs & Toads
pp. 124–25

Turtles
p. 126

Lizards
pp. 127–28

Snakes
pp. 129–30

# California Newt

### *Taricha torosa*

**Length:** 5–8 in

The California newt lives a dual lifestyle as a terrestrial, nonbreeding eft before becoming an aquatic newt. As a terrestrial eft in late summer and fall, it hides under logs and in rock crevices; then at the first rains of winter, it migrates to the water and, upon entering, transforms into an aquatic newt and breeds. • It announces its toxicity to predators by showing off its bright orange underbelly, which it displays by arching its back, raising its head and pointing its tail and legs upward. **Where found:** moist forests from sea level into the Coast ranges.

# Long-toed Salamander

### *Ambystoma macrodactylum*

**Length:** 3–5 in

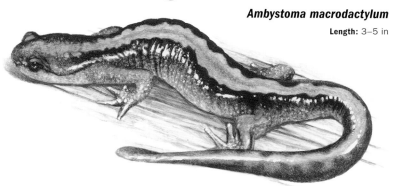

These striking, secretive creatures often hide under rocks or decomposing logs. They feed on invertebrates and are active primarily at night. They are more easily seen in the rainy months of April and May, when they migrate to their breeding sites in silt-free ponds and lakes. Eggs laid singly or in clumps on rocks or vegetation take about 3 weeks to hatch. • There are 2 other common Pacific Northwest salamanders of this genus: the northwestern salamander (*A. gracile*) and the tiger salamander (*A. tigrinum*). **Where found:** arid, low-elevation sagebrush, valley wetlands and subalpine forests; the only salamander to exist on both sides of the Cascade Mountains.

# Coastal Giant Salamander

*Dicamptodon tenebrosus*

**Length:** 7–11½ in

Unlike most salamanders, which are typically nocturnal, coastal giant salamanders often crawl about the forest floor during daylight hours. They have been known to climb trees and shrubs up to 8 ft. • They may give a low-pitched alarm call when captured, but although scars on their tails indicate battles with each other, these large salamanders rarely bite people. **Where found:** moist forests along mountain streams and lakes.

# Van Dyke's Salamander

*Plethodon vandykei*

**Length:** 2½–4½ in

This type of salamander is a lungless salamander, meaning that instead of breathing with lungs, it breathes through its thin, moist skin. It belongs to a family of salamanders called Plethodontidae, which means "many teeth." • The rare Van Dyke's salamander is endemic to western Washington. **Where found:** damp coniferous forests; near or along lakes, streams, springs and seepage areas; northwest coast and western Cascades with 3 isolated populations occupying the Olympic Peninsula, the Willapa Hills and the south Cascades range. **Also known as:** Washington salamander.

123

# Great Basin Spadefoot

### *Spea intermontana*

**Length:** 1½–2½ in

Named for the dark, wedge-shaped "spade" found near the heel of their hind feet, spadefoot toads burrow underground during the day and resurface at night to hunt for insects. A small hump between their eyes, called a boss, protects their heads when pushing their way through the soil to the surface. • These relatively smooth-skinned amphibians are not true toads because they lack parotid glands and warts; instead, they have small, lumpy, black and red tubercles on olive-green to grayish green skin. **Where found:** arid regions east of the Cascades.

# Western Toad

### *Bufo boreas*

**Length:** 2–5 in

Touching a toad will not give you warts, but the western toad does have a way of discouraging our unwanted affections: when handled, it secretes a toxin from large parotid glands behind its eyes that acts to irritate the mouth of potential predators. • This gray, green or brown, large toad is a voracious predator of insects and other tasty invertebrates such as worms and slugs. **Where found:** near springs, streams, meadows and woodlands throughout western regions.

# Coastal Tailed Frog

### *Ascaphus truei*

**Length:** 1–2 in

Frigid mountain streams do not deter these tough little frogs. They lay their eggs on the downstream side of large rocks in fast-flowing streams to prevent them from being swept away in the current, and the tadpoles fastidiously cling to rocks with their suction cup–like mouths. • The adults vary in color from green to gray, brown or reddish brown. The "tail" is actually the male copulatory organ; these frogs are one of the very few frog species with internal fertilization. **Where found:** cold, fast-flowing mountain streams.

# Bullfrog

### *Rana catesbeiana*

**Length:** up to 8 in

Bullfrogs are not native to Washington and Oregon but were introduced in the early 1900s. They are very large and long-living frogs, averaging a 7–9-year lifespan, with records in captivity of individuals living to 16 years. • Bullfrogs are predatory, eating anything they can swallow, including certain snakes and fish, and are incredibly prolific, making them a significant threat to native frog populations. **Where found:** warm, still, shallow, vegetated waters of lakes, ponds, rivers and bogs.

# Red-legged Frog

### *Rana aurora*

**Length:** 2–5½ in

Once hunted for its prized legs for culinary purposes, this frog is now heavily preyed upon by bullfrogs, but habitat loss and water pollution are the red-legged frog's greatest threats. Recent population declines as well as deformities in frogs worldwide have raised public awareness about environmental health. Sightings of this threatened native frog should be reported to the U.S. Fish and Wildlife Service. **Where found:** deep, still or slow-moving ponds or intermittent streams with emergent riparian vegetation; west of the Cascades.

# Pacific Treefrog

### *Hyla regilla*

**Length:** 1–2 in

Pacific treefrogs have adhesive toe pads that enable them to climb vertical surfaces and cling to the tiniest branch. The frogs can also change color within a few minutes, allowing them to blend into their immediate habitat. Colors include green, brown, gray, tan, reddish and black; dark spots are often present. Despite their name, they are often terrestrial, choosing moist, grassy habitat. • The Pacific treefrog was adopted as Washington's state amphibian in 2007. **Where found:** low-elevation shrubby areas close to water; riparian areas. **Also known as:** *Pseudacris regilla*.

125

# Western Pond Turtle

### *Clemmys marmorata*

**Length:** 4–9 in

Unless they see you first and quickly disappear into the water, western pond turtles are typically seen either singly or in groups, basking in the sun on a rock or log in a pond. • Pond turtles feed mainly on crayfish, insects, amphibian eggs and larvae and aquatic plants. Raccoons, large fish and bullfrogs prey on pond turtle eggs and juveniles, but once the turtles mature, predation rates drop significantly. They can live over 50 years in the wild. **Where found:** mud-bottomed ponds, lakes, sloughs, marshes and slow-moving rivers of valleys; along quiet pools of faster-flowing rocky tributaries. **Also known as:** mud turtle.

# Painted Turtle

### *Chrysemys picta*

**Length:** 4–10 in

The bright red belly (plastron, technically speaking) and the distinct yellow stripes on the head and legs are brilliant diagnostics for identifying this striking turtle. • Its mainly vegetarian diet is supplemented with invertebrates, amphibian larvae and small fish. **Where found:** shallow, mud-bottomed water bodies with abundant plant growth, logs and cattail mats; open banks along sluggish rivers with oxbows; sloughs, ponds, lakes and marshes; east of the Cascade Mountains below 3500 ft.

# Sagebrush Lizard

### *Sceloporus graciosus*

**Length:** 1½–5½ in

Sagebrush lizards hunt insects, spiders, mites and ticks on the ground or in shrubs and bask on sun-warmed rocks or hide in shady bushes to maintain their body temperature; studies report lizards allowing themselves to overheat in hot sun to induce a form of fever to break bacterial infections. • Males have blue belly patches and mottling on the throat; the pink sides and neck become brighter on females during breeding season. Sagebrush lizards do not have large, pointed dorsal scales typical of *Sceloporus* species. **Where found:** dry areas with sagebrush; both sides of the Cascades.

# Western Fence Lizard

### *Sceloporus occidentalis*

**Length:** 7 in

Bright blue patches on the sides of the abdomen and under the throat (though on the female, this coloring can be faded or lacking) as well as prickly looking scales on the back are diagnostic of the western fence lizard. The males flaunt their bright blue bellies during breeding season in much the same way that many gloriously plumed male birds do to impress the female and out-rival other males, with which they will aggressively fight. **Where found:** open, sunny areas with logs, fence posts or rocks to bask on; valleys, mountains, oak woodlands and coastal areas west of the Cascades. **Also known as:** blue-bellied lizard.

# Common Side-blotched Lizard

### *Uta stansburiana*

**Length:** 5 in

This lizard is one of the first to be seen in the early hours of dawn, scampering between bushes or perched on rocks. It can be approached quite closely, but it will respond with head bobbing actions that mean to warn off intruders. • With a fairly thin, flat body, this lizard warms quickly and is fueled by the heat of the sun, becoming more active as the temperature rises. The male has a distinctive black blotch on its side, just behind its foreleg. **Where found:** open deserts and sparse juniper woodlands below 6000 ft; arid to semi-arid areas; throughout most of the interior plateau country of the Northwest; south-central Washington and southeastern and central Oregon.

# Pygmy Short-horned Lizard

### *Phrynosoma douglasii*

**Length:** up to 3½ in

This lizard shows a great diversity in coloration because individuals develop coloration matching that of the substrate on which they live: reddish in areas with red, iron-rich soils; pale beige in areas with light, sandy soils or sandstone; and nearly white on the dry lake beds of the Christmas Valley area of Oregon's Lake County. **Where found:** sagebrush areas and juniper and pine woodlands; rocky areas of mountains up to 6000 ft; throughout most of the dry interior plateau country and the mountainous areas of eastern and central Washington and Oregon.

# Western Skink

### *Eumeces skiltonianus*

**Length:** 7½ in

The juvenile western skink sports a bright blue tail that, when grabbed by predators, easily breaks off and continues to writhe while the skink makes its escape; it will soon grow a new tail. An adult's tail fades from blue, becoming reddish orange during breeding season. • Skinks feed on insects and spiders. **Where found:** among leaf litter and underneath bark and rocks; burrows in grasslands; dry oak woodlands west of the Cascades; east of the Cascades, juniper and sagebrush areas and mountain pine forests up to 7000 ft.

# Northern Alligator Lizard

### *Elgaria coerulea*

**Length:** 10 in

The northern alligator lizard feeds on insects, spiders, centipedes, millipedes, ticks, slugs and worms. It lives in cool, shady forests of the north and bears 2–8 live young in summer. • There are 2 subspecies of this lizard in our area, varying in coloration and size and separated by range except in southwestern Oregon, where ranges overlap and hybrids have been observed. **Where found:** coniferous forests; tolerant of cooler climes and elevations up to 7000 ft but seeks out sunny areas; the only lizard along the coast from northern Oregon north, but absent from the Olympic Peninsula; from the Cascades west and in northeastern Washington.

# Rubber Boa

### *Charina bottae*

**Length:** 15–30 in

The rubbery appearance of this snake is owing to its small, smooth dorsal scales and soft, loose skin. It is sometimes called the "two-headed snake" because its head and the tip of its tail have the same thickness and coloring. • Like most constrictors, the rubber boa is an excellent climber and strangles its prey, which includes lizards, amphibians, birds and small mammals. Its defensive posture is to roll up into a ball, hiding its head. **Where found:** under logs or rocks; in grassy openings among trees in wooded areas and coniferous forests at lower elevations.

# Yellow-bellied Racer

### *Coluber constrictor*

**Length:** 2–7 ft

The racer relies on speed to catch prey and escape danger. On the ground, it moves with its head held high for a better view of the terrain; it will also climb shrubs to find birds and insects. • Certain individuals have a bluish caste to the body. The young have large, dark saddles on their backs and faint blotches on their sides. **Where found:** open forests, wooded hills, grassy ditches and riparian areas; oak, chaparral and grassy savannah regions west of Cascades; open juniper and pine forests, rocky canyons and sagebrush flats east of Cascades.

# Ring-necked Snake

### *Diadophis punctatus*

**Length:** 8–30 in; average less than 18 in

Despite its outstanding good looks, this snake is shy and prefers to hide beneath rocks, logs, bark or wood planks and leaf debris. If it is discovered and threatened, it will show its brightly colored underside by coiling its tail upward like a fiery corkscrew, hide its head beneath its body and emit a pungent musk. **Where found:** mixed oak and conifer woodlands, brushy chaparral country and borders of grassy savannahs in scattered populations in the western regions; riparian areas and mountain forests farther east.

# Gophersnake

### *Pituophis catenifer*
Length: 2½–6 ft

This large, beautiful constrictor is often mistaken for a rattlesnake because of its similar coloration, patterning and aggressive defensive strategy. When threatened, it hisses and vibrates its tail against vegetation, often producing a rattling sound. • The gophersnake frequently overwinters in communal dens with other snakes, including rattlesnakes, garter snakes and racers. **Where found:** open, dry, oak savannahs, brushy chaparral, meadows and sparse, sunny areas in coniferous forests and agricultural areas. **Also known as:** bullsnake.

# Common Gartersnake

### *Thamnophis sirtalis*
Length: 20–51 in

Swift on land and in water, the common garter snake is an efficient hunter of amphibians, fish, small mammals, slugs and leeches. Some populations have shown resistance to the toxins produced by the western toad and the California newt and will prey upon them as well. • A single female can give birth to a litter of 3–83, but typically no more than 18, young. **Where found:** aquatic habitats throughout the Pacific Northwest from sea level to just over 7000 ft.

# Western Rattlesnake

### *Crotalus viridus*
Length: average 16–36 in; up to 4 ft and rarely to 5 ft

The subspecies of western rattlesnake that lives in our region is the northern Pacific rattlesnake (*C. v. oreganus*). • Generally unappreciated by humans, the rattlesnake plays an important ecological role, preying upon rodents and other small mammals. It is the only venomous reptile native to the Northwest and has a distinctive, infamous rattle at the end of its tail. The painful rattlesnake bite is rarely lethal to an adult unless untreated for several hours. • Rattlesnakes are born live with a "button" rattle, to which an additional segment is added with each molt. **Where found:** dry areas east of the Cascades.

# FISH

Fish are ectothermic vertebrates that live in the water, have streamlined bodies covered in scales, and possess fins and gills. A fundamental feature of fish is the serially repeated set of vertebrae and segmented muscles that allow the animal to move from side to side, propelling it through the water. A varying number of fins (depending on the species) further aid the fish to swim and navigate. Most fish are oviparous and lay eggs that are fertilized externally. Eggs are either produced in vast quantities and scattered, or they are laid in a spawning nest (redd) under rocks or logs. Parental care may be present in the defence of such a nest or territory. Spawning can involve migrating vast distances back to freshwater spawning grounds after spending 2–3 years in the ocean.

Salmon & Trout
pp. 132–33

Prickleback
p. 133

Goby
p. 134

Rockfish
p. 134

Lingcod
p. 134

Sculpin
p. 135

Sanddab
p. 135

# Chinook Salmon

*Oncorhynchus tshawytscha*

**Length:** 2½–5 ft

The chinook salmon is the largest North American salmon, weighing up to 126 lb and making it a popular sport fish. Most salmon, born as far inland as Idaho, spend a year in freshwater and then travel up to 900 mi to the Pacific Ocean. After 3 years in the ocean, they return to their place of birth to spawn and then die. • During spawning, males have a slightly humped back and a hooked jaw, and they turn dark red to black with a greenish head. • In 1961, the chinook salmon was declared Oregon's state fish. **Where found:** saltwater and freshwater habitats.

# Cutthroat Trout

*Oncorhynchus clarki*

**Length:** 8–12 in

Named for the red streaking in the skin under the lower jaw, cutthroat trout seen in the water can be mistakenly identified as the similar-looking rainbow trout. The cutthroat's reddish belly and throat become brighter during spawning. Females excavate spawning nests (redds) with their tails in late spring or early summer. • There are several subspecies of cutthroat; some populations are coastal, others are freshwater residents and some travel between the brackish estuaries and the freshwater tributaries. **Where found:** saltwater and freshwater habitats.

# Rainbow Trout

*Oncorhynchus mykiss*

**Length:** 7½–18 in

Native to much of western North America and declared Washington's state fish in 1969, this popular fish has been introduced worldwide. Rainbow trout is an important prey species for mink and river otter. • A form of rainbow trout called the steelhead is born in freshwater rivers and streams and migrates to the ocean like salmon. • When spawning, this trout has a greenish to bluish back, silvery sides, a belly often tinged with yellow and green and a reddish lateral line. **Where found:** lakes and streams at most elevations.

# Brook Trout

### *Salvelinus fontinalis*

**Length:** 10 in

Colorful and feisty, the
brook trout is a prized
sport fish introduced
from eastern North America. It is known
to interbreed with other species of trout, and strong management practices must
be put into place to protect native fish. • Brook trout are a type of char. They are
fall spawners and are capable of reproducing in the substrate of high mountain
lakes, whereas other trout species require clean gravel beds in flowing water.
**Where found:** freshwater habitats; widespread throughout the mountain lakes.

# Brown Trout

### *Salmo trutta*

**Length:** 18–35 in

The brown trout
was introduced to the
United States in 1893 from Europe.
Its large size and adaptability have made it a popular sport fish throughout the
world. • Like most other trout, it spawns in fall and eats aquatic invertebrates.
A brown trout will also eat the occasional amphibian or small mammal that
ventures into the water. Its color ranges from golden brown to olive. **Where found:**
freshwater habitats; streams, ponds, lakes and reservoirs.

# Black Prickleback

### *Xiphister atropurpureus*

**Length:** up to 12 in

Although it looks and acts similar
to an eel, the black prickleback is
not a true eel. It often slithers out
of water under rocks and seaweed,
able to breathe air out of water for
10 hours or longer as long as it stays
relatively moist. • The breeding pair
fastidiously fertilizes each of their
738–4070 eggs individually, adding them
one by one to a cluster! **Where found:** saltwater habitats; close to rocky shores with
algal cover; tide pools, lower intertidal and shallow subtidal zones down to depths
of 26 ft; under rocks and in gravel areas. **Also known as:** black blenny.

# Blackeye Goby

### *Coryphopterus nicholsi*

**Length:** up to 6 in

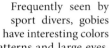

Frequently seen by sport divers, gobies have interesting colors and patterns and large eyes. The blackeye goby is less colorful than many other gobies, but it has distinctive black, bulbous eyes that contrast with its pale body. A black border to the dorsal fin (and pectoral fin of breeding males) is a diagnostic feature. • It lays 500–3000 eggs over the spawning season and is very territorial toward other blackeye gobies near its nest. **Where found:** saltwater habitats; sand- and mud-bottomed waters near rocky areas and reefs and in bays as well as in deep waters.

# Blue Rockfish

### *Sebastes mystinus*

**Length:** up to 21 in

Significant numbers of these fish are claimed by sport fishing each year; their wild predators include seals and sea-lions. Predation on eggs is reduced by female rockfish carrying the eggs internally until just before they are ready to hatch. • Blue rockfish are sometimes found in large groups feeding on jellyfish, smaller fish and crustaceans. They can also be found among rocky reefs, where they are a popular subject of underwater photography; their sedentary behavior makes it seem like they actually pose for the camera. **Where found:** salt-water habitats; rocky reefs in both shallow and deep waters; kelp beds.

# Lingcod

### *Ophiodon elongatus*

**Length:** up to 5 ft

Larger farther north in their range, the largest ling-cod on record was from British Columbia, weighing in at 105 lb; the average in our area weighs half that figure. It is a highly prized sport-fish and popular for eating by humans and sea lions. • This spiny, unfriendly looking fish is very territorial; males vigilantly guard nests containing egg masses 2 ft across. **Where found:** saltwater habitats; seasonal migration between shallow and deep waters to 1500 ft. *Adult:* rocky reefs and kelp. *Juvenile:* sandy or muddy bays.

# Tidepool Sculpin

### *Oligocottus maculosus*

Length: 3½ in

Sculpins are famous for their looks—they're so ugly that they're cute. Bulging eyes, fat, wide lips, roughly textured skin with mottled coloration and dorsal spines add up to one visually impressive fish. • An individual tidepool sculpin tends to select one particular tide pool to call home and will return to it if displaced. **Where found:** saltwater habitats; sheltered intertidal areas; tide pools.

# Pacific Sanddab

### *Citharichthys sordidus*

Length: up to 16 in

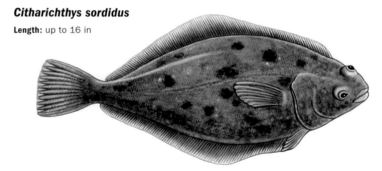

The Pacific sanddab is a type of flatfish that hides in the sand at the seafloor. Its flat body and cryptic coloration keep this fish almost invisible with only a thin layer of sand atop it. • Although born with an eye on either side of its head, the Pacific sanddab spends its life lying on its right side, resulting in both its eyes shifting to the left (top) side of its body (occasionally an individual will lie to the other side). • It is a highly sought-after fish commercially as well as by anglers. **Where found:** saltwater habitats; soft, sandy ocean floors.

# INVERTEBRATES

**M**ore than 95% of all animal species on the planet are invertebrates, and there are thousands of invertebrate species in Washington and Oregon. The few mentioned in this guide are frequently encountered and easily recognizable. Invertebrates can be found in a variety of habitats and are an important part of most ecosystems. They provide food for birds, amphibians, shrews, bats and other insects, and they also play an important role in the pollination of plants and aid in the decay process.

Seashells
pp. 138–39

Sea Slug
p. 140

Sea Cucumber
p. 140

Sea Stars
pp. 140–41

Sand Dollar & Sea Urchin
p. 141

Anemones, Coral & Sponge
pp. 142–43

Jellyfish
p. 143

Octopus
p. 143

Crustaceans
pp. 144–45

Butterflies & Moths
pp. 146–47

Dragonflies
pp. 148–49

Beetles
pp. 149–50

Wasps & Bees
p. 150

Ants
p. 151

Crane Flies & Lacewings
p. 151

Aquatic Insects
p. 152

Non-Insect Arthropods
pp. 152–53

Slug
p. 153

# Black Tegula

### *Tegula funebralis*

**Length:** 1 in

These snails are some of the most abundant on the Pacific Coast. Large individuals are known to live 20–30 years. They take advantage of sloped substrates to flee predators such as sea stars by pulling inside their shells and rolling away. • Empty black tegula shells are a favorite home acquisition of hermit crabs. **Where found:** rocky shores between high- and low-tide lines. **Also known as:** turban tegula, black turban snail.

# Lewis' Moon Snail

### *Polinices lewisii*

**Length:** 3½ in

The large, gray foot and mantle that covers most of its shell are characteristic of this large, almost round snail. • Lewis' moon snail preys on small clams it finds in the mud and feeds by wrapping its foot around them, drilling a hole into the clam shell with its radula and chewing out the contents. This method of feeding explains the small holes often found in clamshells that wash up on the beach. **Where found:** sand and sand-mud substrates; intertidal zones, sandy flats and bays with quiet waters.

# Pacific Razor Clam

### *Siliqua patula*

**Length:** 7 in

Prized by commercial fisheries, this clam is a favorite of seafood enthusiasts. Clam diggers do not have to dig deep to collect this mollusk, but they must be prepared to get wet. The Pacific razor clam does not dig a permanent burrow; instead, it moves about with the waves and continuously digs shallow holes in the sand until it is ready to catch the next good wave. • A razor clam can live 18 years, though it typically doesn't survive more than 5 years before being preyed upon. **Where found:** near the low-tide line and in shallow water all along the coast.

# California Mussel

### *Mytilus californianus*

**Length:** 10 in

California mussels are the most conspicuous and abundant animals on our shores. They are predominant in the upper tidal zone and occur in massive growths. Mussels are capable of limited locomotion but rarely move from their practically permanent position; they attach to a substrate by byssal threads produced by their foot. • Sea stars, crabs, shorebirds and sea otters are among their top predators, but the supreme enthusiast for this tasty mollusk is human. **Where found:** on rocks, wharf pilings and unprotected shores; from well above the low-tide line to water 80 ft deep.

# Gumboot Chiton

### *Cryptochiton stelleri*

**Length:** 13 in; up to 16 in

The fleshy girdle that covers the shell of the gumboot chiton makes it less attractive than the more glamorous lined chiton, but this chiton is impressive in other ways. The gumboot chiton is the world's largest chiton and is found in relative abundance right here on our shores. Another amazing fact about this massive mollusk is that it can live 20 years or longer. **Where found:** on rocks in protected waters near deep channels and in kelp beds; from the low-tide line to depths of 70 ft. **Also known as:** Pacific giant chiton.

# Lined Chiton

### *Tonicella lineata*

**Length:** 2 in

The gorgeous lined chiton sports an array of fashionable shells typically mottled reddish brown as a background and decorated with zigzag lines patterned across it in colors varying from light and dark reds to blues or browns to black or white. The fleshy girdle that surrounds the 8-sectioned plate of armor (chitons are the only mollusk with jointed shells) is usually a greenish or yellowish color. **Where found:** on rocks covered with coralline algae; underneath purple sea urchins; from the low-tide line to depths of 180 ft.

# Sea Lemon

### *Anisodoris nobilis*

**Length:** 10 in

Nudibranchs are poor swimmers; instead, they crawl along the ocean floor with a strong, suction-like foot common to all slug species of gastropods. • The sea lemon feeds entirely upon sponges. It has a fruity (lemony according to some) scent that is apparently repellant to predators. • The sea lemon has 2 antenna-like rhinophores at its anterior end, a circular, many-branched cluster of gills on the posterior end and is covered in short, rounded tubercles everywhere in between. **Where found:** on pilings, around docks and on rocks below the low-tide line. **Also known as:** noble Pacific doris.

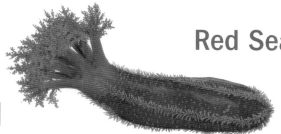

# Red Sea Cucumber

### *Cucumaria miniata*

**Length:** 10 in

Typically bright red, but also orange, pink or purple, this long, smooth, highly tentacled sea cucumber nestles in crevices and under rocks within moving water currents. It has 10 main retractable tentacles of equal length, each highly branched at the ends, and 5 rows of tube feet along its length. • Sea cucumbers are detritivores, feeding on dead and decaying organic material. • As a defense mechanism, and no doubt effectively repulsive, sea cucumbers can spit out their guts and regenerate them. **Where found:** near the low-tide line and in shallow depths in circulating waters.

# Bat Star

### *Patiria miniata*

**Radius:** 6–8 in

Bat stars are the most abundant sea stars on the West Coast. This species is highly variable in color—from reddish orange to purple to green, often with mottled patterns—and form, with 5 (sometimes 4–9) short, thick arms. • Sea stars feed upon bivalves, wrapping around them and forcing them out of their shells, and will scavenge dead fish. Their predators are other sea stars, mollusks and crustaceans, but predators are often deterred by bat stars' secretions of distasteful chemicals. **Where found:** kelp forests; on rocks or sand from the low-tide line to depths of 960 ft.

# Ochre Sea Star

### *Pisaster ochraceus*

**Radius:** 10 in

Beautiful yellow, orange, brown, reddish or purple ochre sea stars often suffer from over-collection by beachcombers who unfortunately do not realize that this color will be lost once the sea star dies and dries up. • Ochre sea stars are an important, keystone predatory species whose absence in an ecosystem causes visible shifts in the numbers, types and dominances of other species. This sea star is abundant on beds of mussels, its favored prey, and is preyed upon by gulls and sea otters. **Where found:** intertidal areas; wave-washed, rocky shores at the low-tide line.

# Eccentric Sand Dollar

### *Dendraster excentricus*

**Radius:** 1½ in

Beachcombers are most familiar with this sand dollar as a smooth, spineless, gray specimen with a 5-petaled flower design in the center of its surface; in its living form, it is furry in appearance and its color varies from light lavender-gray to brown or reddish brown to a dark, almost black, purple. • Eccentric sand dollars colonize sandy ocean floors, stabilizing the strata. In rough waters, they will bury themselves under the sand for protection. • Sand dollars are closely related to sea urchins. **Where found:** sandy bottoms of sheltered bays and open coasts; from the low-tide line to depths of 130 ft.

# Purple Sea Urchin

### *Strongylocentrotus purpuratus*

**Radius:** 2 in without spines

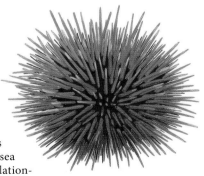

In large populations, the purple sea urchin and the red sea urchin (*S. franciscanus*) are capable of overgrazing and destroying the important kelp forests, a situation that a healthy population of sea otters, the urchin's main predator, keeps in check. Sea urchins, sea otters and kelp forests maintain a tight interrelationship and all require unpolluted waters. • Adult purple sea urchins are a vivid purple, but the juveniles are green. **Where found:** from the low-tide line and rocky shores into kelp forests in waters up to 300 ft deep.

# Aggregating Anemone

### *Anthopleura elegantissima*

**Height:** *Aggregating individuals:* 6 in;
*Solitary individuals:* 20 in
**Width:** *Aggregating individuals:* 3 in;
*Solitary individuals:* 10 in

This sea anemone has 5 rings of tentacles with tips varying in delicate colors of pink, lavender and blue. The aggregating form is in fact a colony of clones created by the "founding" anemone dividing itself in a form of asexual reproduction. These clones tolerate proximity to each other because they are not competing genetically; if a genetically different individual was in proximity, they would lash out with their tentacles, wounding or killing it. Their toxins are completely benign to their clones. **Where found:** rock walls, boulders or pilings from intertidal to low-tide zones.

# Giant Green Anemone

### *Anthoplerua xanthogrammica*

**Height:** 12 in
**Width:** 10 in

The giant green anemone is a solitary green giant, but it is not anti-social; often within tentacle-tip distance to another, it makes contact every once in a while as if to reassure itself that is it not alone. • Its green column varies to brown, and its thick, short, tapered tentacles vary from green to blue to white in rows of 6 or more. The green coloring is enhanced by a symbiotic relationship with green algae and protists, from which the anemone obtains photosynthetic byproducts. **Where found:** exposed coastlines; on rocks, seawalls and pilings in tide pools and down to depths of more than 50 ft.

# Orange Cup Coral

### *Balanophyllia elegans*

**Height:** ½ in
**Width:** ½ in

This is the only stony coral in the intertidal zone of the Pacific coast from British Columbia to Baja California. Stony coral has a stony, cup-shaped skeleton in which the base of the animal is set, and 36 long, tapered, translucent tentacles reach out and contract back within the skeleton. The tentacles have masses of stinging cells dotted along them, so do not be tempted to touch this lovely, bright orange beauty. The fluorescent pigment is bright even at depths of 30 ft or more. **Where found:** shaded waters such as under ledges and boulders from the low-tide line down to depths of 70 ft; all along the coast.

# Purple Sponge

### *Haliclona permollis*

**Height:** 1½ in
**Width:** 36 in

Looking like a bubblegum-colored lava spill, this
encrusting sponge pours itself over rocks and within
tide pools. Its smooth, soft form seems to bubble with little raised volcanoes up to
¼ in higher than the surface of the sponge. • Sponges reproduce either by budding
(a tip is released or breaks off and regenerates upon attachment to a new site) or by
releasing tiny clusters of cells that germinate on a new site. Sponges are also capable
of sexual reproduction, releasing sperm into the water that then fertilizes eggs in
another sponge; the larvae swim to a new site, attach and develop into a tiny sponge.
**Where found:** sheltered waters from the intertidal zone to depths of 20 ft.

# Moon Jellyfish

### *Aurelia aurita*

**Radius:** 7½ in

This ethereal, whitish to translucent medusa
is a favorite food of the leatherback sea turtle
but not a favored acquaintance of swimmers
and snorkelers—a jellyfish can give a painful
sting, and it also releases polyps in the water that
are very difficult to see but easily felt. The sting may cause a slight rash or itching for
several hours. • The moon jellyfish has 8 lobes fringed by numerous short tentacles
and 4 long, oral arms, also with frilly margins. **Where found:** floats near the surface
just offshore and often washes up on beaches during high tide or after a storm.

# Red Octopus

### *Octopus rubescens*

**Armspread:** up to 18 in

Octopi are extremely advanced invertebrates
that possess many clever behaviors that are a
constant source of entertainment for divers
and snorkelers; their ability to squirt screens of
ink and change the color and texture of their
skin to camouflage against their surroundings are
among the most impressive. Their camouflaging skills, however, make
them challenging to identify. The red octopus is in fact often sandy beige to blend
in with the sand outside of its den, which is noticeable by the deposits of its many
lobster (and other invertebrate) dinners. **Where found:** sandy habitats in shallow
waters close to shore out to depths of 600 ft.

# Giant Acorn Barnacle

### *Balanus nubilus*

**Radius:** up to 2 in

We typically see this barnacle closed, but, though rarely and sometimes not for months at a time, when it feeds, long, feathery plumes reach out from the top of the barnacle shell to filter bits of organic matter from the water. • This barnacle is intolerant of exposure and must remain almost continuously covered by water, or it will easily desiccate. • Capable of sexual reproduction yet immobile, this animal has the largest penis-to-body size ratio so that the male can reach his mate. **Where found:** rocky shores and exposed coasts; lower intertidal areas with continuous water cover; subtidal to depths of 300 ft.

# Barred Shrimp

### *Heptacarpus pugettensis*

**Length:** up to 1 in

*Heptacarpus* species are the "broken-back" shrimps, named for the distinctive kink in their backs. There are many species in quite high numbers along our coast, but they are not often noticeable as they lay motionless in bright daylight hours, their translucent coloring blending them into the substrate. Disturb still tide pool waters and watch them scurry. **Where found:** from the low-tide line to depths of 50 ft.

# Dungeness Crab

### *Cancer magister*

**Length:** 6½ in

These crabs are the most sought-after species for commercial harvest on the Pacific Coast south of Alaska. Dungeness crabs are usually only found in water around 100 ft deep, but they come to shallow water to molt their shells, which do not grow with the crabs as they do with other species that have exoskeletons. The molted shells often wash up onto the beach. **Where found:** sand bottoms from the low-tide line to water more than 300 ft deep.

# Purple Shore Crab

### *Hemigrapsus nudus*

**Length:** 2 in

The purple shore crab scuttles sideways about rocky shorelines scavenging animal matter and grazing on the film of algae growing on the rocks. It hides under rocks and burrows under mud for shelter and is quite tolerant of remaining dry for extended periods without desiccating. **Where found:** open, rocky shores; among seaweeds in shallow, protected waters.

# Blue-handed Hermit Crab

### *Pagurus samuelis*

**Length:** ¾ in

The blue-handed hermit crab does not produce its own shell, and only the front portion of its body is armored; it must protect the soft regions of its body by acquiring a discarded snail shell. The black tegula shell is one of the preferred shells for this little crab to make a home. If the crab outgrows its current shell or finds a more suitable and otherwise unoccupied shell, it will relocate. **Where found:** open, rocky shores; permanent tide pools; from the intertidal zone subtidal to depths of 50 ft.

145

# Western Tiger Swallowtail

### *Papilio rutulus*

**Wingspan:** 3¼–3½ in

The "tail" of the swallowtail is defensive, strategizing that if a bird is to attack, it will grab at this extension, in which event the butterfly's body will be spared. This butterfly is often seen with the lower half of its wings missing, implying that the strategy must indeed work. • The western tiger swallowtail never seems go unnoticed or without a compliment from its observer. The caterpillar is also stunning, sporting a smooth, green body with bright yellow and blue eyespots at one end; it feeds upon poplar trees. **Where found:** along watercourses and in gardens.

# Spring Azure

### *Celastrina argiolus*

**Wingspan:** 1–1½ in

This dainty, blue butterfly is one of the first butterflies to announce the arrival of spring. It feeds on the buds and flowers of spring blooms on mountain shrubs. An adult lives for only 1–2 weeks, in which time it must breed and lay its eggs. The larvae often develop on the leaves of dogwood and cherry trees and may be tended to and protected by ants for the sweet "honeydew" that they produce. **Where found:** from lush valley bottoms to high alpine meadows.

# Clouded Sulphur, Orange Sulphur

### *Colias philodice, C. eurytheme*

**Wingspan:** 1½–2 in

Differing from each other mainly in color between yellow and orange, the many species of sulphur are all very tricky to tell apart. • Like all other butterflies, sulphurs play a vital role in pollinating many wild plants. Attracted to flowers by their brilliantly colored petals, butterflies obtain nectar with their long, coilable proboscis and meanwhile are sprinkled with fine, sticky pollen, which they carry to the next plant. **Where found:** meadows, fields and vegetated roadsides; from low-elevation valleys to subalpine areas.

# Pacific Fritillary

**Boloria epithore**

**Wingspan:** 1½ in

Fritillaries are a group of orange and black butterflies. Lesser fritillaries, such as the Pacific fritillary, are smaller than the greater fritillaries and do not have the typical silver spots on their underwings that the greater fritillaries do.

• The lesser fritillaries are noticeable for spreading their wings while they feed, rather than folding them atop their backs. For this reason, they are a favorite subject for nature photographers. **Where found:** meadows and clearings.

# Mourning Cloak

**Nymphalis antiopa**

**Wingspan:** 3 in

Mourning cloaks are one of the longest-living butterflies, living for up to a full year (most butterflies live mere days or weeks, rarely months) and are tolerant of cool temperatures. Adults emerge from their pupae in mid- to late summer and may over-winter under bark, debris or even a window shutter, but if temperatures are above freezing, they can be seen even in winter. They emerge from hibernation in spring to mate and lay eggs. • The caterpillars feed with enthusiasm on aspen and willow trees. **Where found:** openings in forested areas.

# Polyphemus Moth

**Antheraea polyphemus**

**Wingspan:** 4¼–4½ in

This large moth is always noticed for its spectacular colors and designs. The large eyespots exist for defensive purposes; if the wings are closed and a predator, such as a bird, approaches, the polyphemus moth will flash its wings open like eyelids to create the illusion that it is a much larger creature and not prey. • Polyphemus was a one-eyed giant in Greek mythology. **Where found:** deciduous forests.

# Common Spreadwing

### *Lestes disjunctus*
**Length:** 1½ in

As an exception to the rule about how dragon-flies and damselflies posture their wings, this damselfly assumes the dragonfly position, thus giving it the name spreadwing. Juveniles have a bit of blue coloring, but as the common spreadwing ages, it becomes iridescent green or brown and is covered in a waxy powder called pruinose that is very much like the waxiness of a plum or prune. Specialists theorize that pruinose adds to the reflectivity of the ultraviolet signals that this insect uses in courtship. **Where found:** near slow-flowing streams.

# Green Darner

### *Anax junius*
**Length:** 3 in

This gorgeous dragonfly is a migratory species, coming into our area from the north in spring. It breeds in the Pacific Northwest in ponds and shallow lakes, and the subsequent generation migrates south for the winter. • The male is mostly blue with a green thorax; the female is green with a gray or brown abdomen. • The green darner was adopted as the state insect of Washington in 1997. **Where found:** near ponds and lakes.

# American Emerald

### *Cordulia shurtleffi*
**Length:** 1¾ in

The American emerald is a beautiful dragonfly of the northern forests. The large, bright green eyes are vivid against its dark, iridescent, coppery jade body. It comes out in large num-bers in the boggy forests in spring to breed and lay its eggs. **Where found:** quiet, still waters of boggy ponds, marshes and shallow lakes.

# Common Whitetail

### *Libellula lydia*

**Length:** 1¾ in

The great diversity of dragonflies and damselflies in the Pacific Northwest allows for a spectacular display of color and pattern in the spring. The common whitetail is yet another lovely example of nature's artistry. It patrols the surface of ponds, gorging itself on mosquitoes—another reason to appreciate this insect. **Where found:** near ponds throughout the Pacific Northwest.

# Variegated Meadowhawk

### *Sympetrum corruptum*

**Length:** 1½ in

Like so much of nature, there is still so much left to learn when it comes to variegated meadowhawks. These widespread dragonflies stage a mass migration on the West Coast in fall. They are observed heading south, but it is yet unknown where they travel to, where they came from prior to congregating *en masse*, or even what triggers them to know when to do so. Some experts are studying whether fall wind patterns give them environmental clues as to their travel date. **Where found:** ponds and lakes; prefer stagnant waters.

# Pacific Tiger Beetle

### *Cicindela oregona*

**Length:** ½ in

The Pacific tiger beetle is not the most colorful of its kind, but it is impressive nonetheless with its powerful jaws and fast movements. It is common, but you have to have a quick eye to see one before it dashes off in hiding. • This beetle preys on other insects and can be seen on the prowl either hunting for its dinner or hunting for a mate. **Where found:** moist sand and gravel alongside rivers and lakes; widespread.

# Convergent Ladybug

### *Hippodamia convergens*

**Length:** ¼ in

There are several species of ladybug, all distinguishable from each other by their size, number of spots and coloration. Some ladybugs are not even red. They emerge from the pupae and do not change their size or the number of spots as they age. • Ladybugs feed, ravenously, on aphids. They can be bought in garden centers to put in a garden with aphid problems; they will have a significant impact, especially in a greenhouse. Once released, most will fly away. **Where found:** open areas and hilltops in spring and fall.

# Yellow Jackets

### *Vespula* spp.

**Length:** ½–¾ in

Amazing engineers of paper architecture, yellow jackets chew on bark or wood and mix it with saliva to make the pulp. Large sheets of paper line the nest in which 6-sided paper chambers hold the larvae. Different types of wood create swirls of color, grays and browns, inadvertently adding some artistic style to the structure. The nest can reach the size of a basketball by the end of summer; only the queen, however, will survive winter—the only safe time of year to get a close-up look at a wasp nest without being stung by one of the architects. **Where found:** nest in high branches or in abandoned animal burrows; widespread. **Also known as:** paper wasp, hornet.

# Bumble Bees

### *Bombus* spp.

**Length:** ¼–¾ in

Bees have long inspired our admiration and appreciation; throughout history, the image of the bee appears on ancient coins, in Masonic, Mormon, Pagan, Jewish, Egyptian and Greek symbology, as an icon of royalty in Sudan, Niger, France and India, as a personal emblem adopted by Napoleon Bonaparte, as a sacred feminine symbol of the Cult of Athena and as an embodiment of the goddess Venus—just to name a few examples! **Where found:** clearings and meadows wherever there are flowering plants.

# Carpenter Ants

**Camponotus spp.**

**Length:** ½ in

Similar but unrelated to termites, carpenter ants bore through wood to construct their homes in trees and sometimes in our wooden homes as well. Watch for a pile of sawdust in either case. • These are the largest ants in our area, and they are preyed upon by our largest woodpeckers, pileated woodpeckers (*Dryocopus pileatus*). • Carpenter ants do not sting as do other species of ant, but their powerful, wood-chewing jaws are capable of a strong bite. **Where found:** forested areas.

# Giant Crane Flies

**Holorusia spp.**

**Length:** up to 1½ in

These innocent insects are not giant mosquitoes or garden harvestmen ("daddy longlegs") but very benign and harmless crane flies. Giant crane flies do not bite, and their larvae only scavenge in soil and rotting logs. • The crane is an appropriate analogy to these long-legged creatures that are more comfortable in the forest than when they accidentally find themselves inside your house. **Where found:** forested areas.

# Green Lacewings

**Chrysopa spp.**

**Length:** ½ in

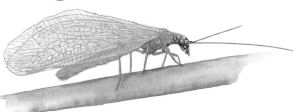

Lacewings are frequent visitors to your garden, where their lime-green bodies camouflage into the light foliage of young plants. They have elegant filigreed wings (hence lacewing), large golden eyes and, if you pick one up, you will notice they produce an odd scent. • Both the adults and larvae of these beneficial insects feed on aphids. **Where found:** shrubby or forested areas and gardens; widespread.

# Stream Skater

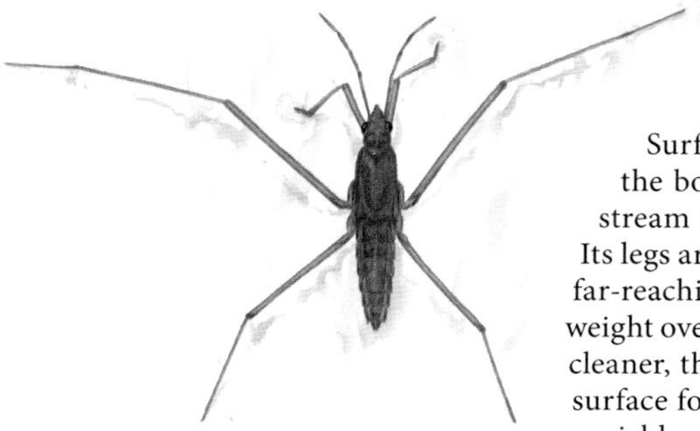

**_Aquaricus remigis_**

Length: ¾ in

Surface tension on water along with the body shape of this insect allows the stream skater to walk, or skate, on water. Its legs are water repellant but also long and far-reaching, thus distributing the skater's weight over a large area. • Like a diligent pool cleaner, the stream skater prowls the water's surface for dead or drowning bugs, which it quickly consumes. **Where found:** streams and small rivers.

# Water Boatman

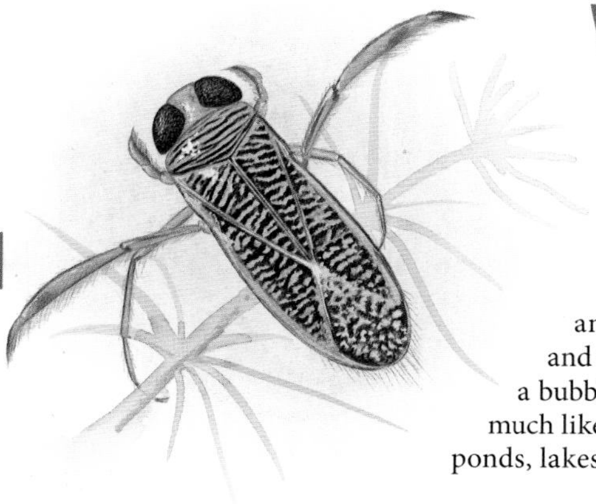

**Family Corixidae**

Length: ¼–½ in

The three sets of legs on the water boatman are each adapted for a specific function: digging in the mud for food, holding on to plants and rocks underwater or swimming and maneuvering. These great divers carry a bubble of air under their abdomens to use much like a primitive scuba tank. **Where found:** ponds, lakes, rivers and streams.

# Garden Centipedes

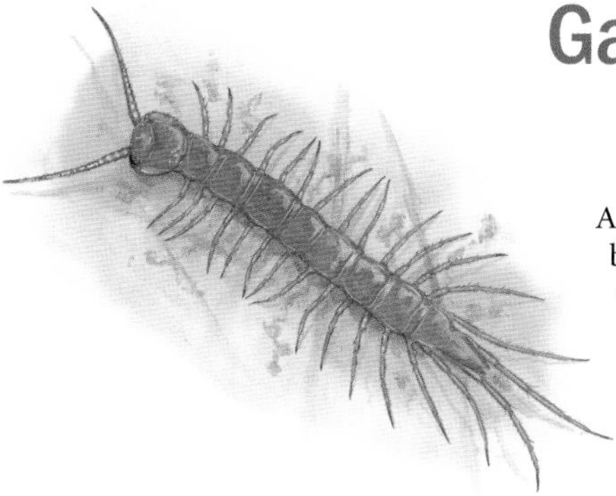

**_Lithobius_ spp.**

Length: up to 1¼ in

A centipede moves its many legs very quickly, but if you manage to see one sitting still, you can count 1 set of legs per body segment—significantly less than 100 feet, as the name suggests. • This predator has venomous fangs with which it subdues its prey. It is not dangerous to people but nevertheless should be avoided, especially by small children. • Centipedes require a moist environment to survive and will quickly desiccate if they find their way into a house. **Where found:** under moist debris or cover in gardens and forests.

# Clown Millipede

### *Harpaphe haydeniana*

**Length:** 1¾ in

Although it has twice as many legs (2 sets per body segment) as the centipede, the millipede moves at least half as fast—actually quite slowly. Because it feeds upon plants and detritus, the clown millipede does not need to move quickly to catch a meal. Its main defense against those animals that would want to prey upon it, such as birds and lizards, is to curl up in a ball and produce cyanide, which has an odor that deters a would-be predator. Some people compare the scent produced by the millipede to almond. **Where found:** forested areas with Douglas-fir. **Also known as:** cyanide millipede.

# Western Black Widow

### *Latrodectus hesperus*

**Length:** *Male:* up to ¼ in; *Female:* up to ½ in

Not known for its web-making skills, the black widow makes a disorga-nized mass of web and lives in the abandoned burrows of small mammals. If seen out of hiding, the western black widow is easy to identify by its shiny, large, black body with a red hourglass on the underside. • It is fairly common knowl-edge that the bite of a black widow is dangerous and best avoided. Also accurate in common knowledge is the fact that the female does most often eat the male after mating, but it is not the only spider to do so. **Where found:** dry, well-drained areas.

# Yellow-orange Banana Slug

### *Ariolimax columbianus*

**Length:** up to 10 in

The largest slug in North America and second-largest in the world, the yellow-orange banana slug often looks quite rightly like a banana on the forest floor, but it can also vary in shade or have mottling of browns and greens. It pos-sesses 2 pairs of retractable tentacles, the longer of which sense the brightness of light and the shorter of which sense smell. • This slug lives 1–7 years. It is an important forest floor decomposer, scavenging organic debris and favoring mush-rooms. **Where found:** under logs or debris on moist forest floors.

# PLANTS

**P**lants belong to the Kingdom Plantae. They are autotrophic, which means that they produce their own food from inorganic materials through a process called photosynthesis. Plants are the basis of all food webs. They supply oxygen to the atmosphere, modify climate, and create and hold down soil. They disperse their seeds and pollen through carriers such as wind or animals. Fossil fuels come from ancient deposits of organic matter—largely that of plants. In this book, plants are separated into 3 categories: trees, shrubs and herbs.

# TREES

Trees are long-lived, woody plants that are normally taller than 16 ft. There are 2 types of trees: coniferous and broadleaf. Conifers, or cone-bearers, have needles or small, scale-like leaves. Most conifers are evergreens, but larches, bald-cypress (*Taxodium distichum*) and dawn redwood (*Metasequoia glyptostroboides*) shed their leaves in winter. Most broadleaf trees lose their leaves in the fall, and are often called deciduous trees (meaning "falling off" in Latin). Some exceptions include rhododendron and several hollies.

Trees are important to various ecosystems. A single tree can provide a home or a food source for many different animals. A group of trees can provide windbreak, camouflage or shelter, hold down soil and control runoff. A forest that is large and diverse in its structure and composition (species variety, understory, age, density) defines the community of species that live within it. The integrity of a forest relies on having a large enough area and a variety of plant species of different ages. Old-growth forest is critical habitat for many species that use the fallen or hollowed out trees as nesting or denning sites. Many species of invertebrates live within or under the bark, providing food for birds. Fallen, decomposing logs provide habitat for mosses, fungi and invertebrates. The logs eventually completely degrade into nutrient-rich soil to perpetuate the continued growth of plant life and retain organic matter in the ecosystem. Large forests retain carbon dioxide, an important preventive factor of global warming, and responsibly managed forests can sustain an industry that provides wood products and jobs.

Firs, Spruces & Pines
pp. 157–61

Yew
p. 162

Redcedar
p. 162

**Oak**
p. 163

**Alder & Birch**
pp. 163–64

**Cottonwood & Aspen**
pp. 164–65

**Cherry**
p. 165

**Madrone**
p. 166

**Dogwood**
p. 166

**Maple**
p. 167

**Ash**
p. 167

# White Fir

### *Abies concolor*

**Height:** 130–180 ft
**Needles:** 2–3 in long
**Seed cones:** 3–5½ in long

Christmas trees are often white fir, with a fragrance that creates nostalgia for the holiday season. Foresters don't often view this tree with the same fondness, because it is shade tolerant and outcompetes sugar pines and incense cedars. In addition, its low-hanging limbs are a fire hazard, inviting small fires to reach up to the canopy and threaten otherwise unreachable trees such as the giant sequoia. • This tree's soft, knotty wood is used commercially only for pulp and cheap construction materials. **Where found:** Klamath Mountains. **Also known as:** amabilis fir, Pacific silver fir.

# Grand Fir

### *Abies grandis*

**Height:** 100–200 ft
**Needles:** 1¼–1⅝ in long, flattened
**Seed cones:** 2–4 in long, yellowish green to green

The fragrant fir has prompted people to burn the needles as incense, hang the boughs as air-fresheners and select it over pine for a Christmas tree (also because firs hold their needles well). Mystically, burning fir needles and wood is believed to chase away bad spirits and ghosts, revive the spirits of people near death, give protection and renewed confidence to people afraid of thunder and lightning and even cure a sick horse! **Where found:** in foothills and montane zones in valleys and along streams; also on dry slopes up to 5000 ft and in shady areas; along the coast and east and west of the Cascades.

# Douglas-fir

### *Pseudotsuga menziesii*

**Height:** 82–130 ft, up to 200 ft,
short rugged forms on the coast
**Needles:** ¾–1¼ in long, aromatic, blunt,
often flattened, in 2 rows
**Seed cones:** 2–4 in long

In Native mythology, mice hid in Douglas-fir cones, and their tails and hind legs can still be seen sticking out from under the scales. • The inner bark and seeds were survival foods for Native groups and pioneers; the young, vitamin C–rich needles were used in teas to treat scurvy; and the sugar crystals that form on the tips of the branches on hot days were a rare treat. • This tree is a top timber producer and makes a fragrant Christmas tree, but if left to grow, a Douglas-fir can live for well over 1000 years. **Where found:** moist to very dry sites; low to mid elevation; Coast and Cascade ranges. **Also known as:** red fir, Oregon pine, Douglas spruce.

# Englemann Spruce

### *Picea engelmannii*

**Height:** 82–100 ft
**Needles:** ¾–1¼ in long
**Seed cones:** 1⅝–2 in long

Narrow, spire-like crowns, whorls of drooping lower branches, and sharp, 4-sided needles help to identify this common, aromatic evergreen. • Native peoples made canoes from the bark and split the roots to make cord and thread. • The lumber often contains small knots but it is still used for home construction, prefabricated products and especially pulp owing to the long, light-colored,  resin-free fibers. Spruce wood is also used for high-end, specialty items such as violins, pianos and aircraft parts. **Where found:** high-elevation forests along the crest and east slope of the Cascades.

# Sitka Spruce

### *Picea sitchensis*

**Height:** 230 ft
**Needles:** ¾–1¼ in long, 4-sided
**Seed cones:** 2–3 in long, reddish brown to brown

Spruce was utilized by Native peoples and early settlers and continues to be valuable today, and the majestic old groves are important ecologically and inspire us with their beauty. The bark, gum, needles, pitch and wood were used for food, tea, medicine, caulking, water sealant, textile and pulp. Spruce beer, said to taste like root beer, was popular among early northern travelers and was important in preventing scurvy. **Where found:** moist, well-drained sites such as floodplains and bogs; more ancient trees occur in low terraces or river floodplains, such as along the Hoh River in Olympic National Park.

# Western Larch

### *Larix occidentalis*

**Height:** 100–180 ft
**Needles:** 1–1½ in long, flattened, turning yellow in fall
**Seed cones:** 1–1¼ in

Larch sap can be evaporated into a type of molasses and mixed with sugar to make syrup. Chewing on the dried sap is said to aid digestion and relieve sore throats, and further studies are investigating the medicinal properties of the polysaccharide comprised of arabinogalatins, which is reputed to stimulate immunity. • The straight, durable and rot-resistant wood is often used for telephone poles, railroad ties, posts, construction timbers, mine timbers and boat-building. **Where found:** well-drained upper foothills and montane; northeastern Washington and north-central Oregon, along the east slopes of the Cascade Mountains and in the Blue and Wallowa Mountains.

# Western Hemlock

## *Tsuga heterophylla*

**Height:** 100–165 ft
**Needles:** ³⁄₈–³⁄₄ in long, flat, blunt, unequal,
in 2 opposite rows
**Seed cones:** ⁵⁄₈–1 in long, numerous

This attractive, feathery tree was declared Washington's state tree in 1991. • These trees are popular as ornamentals, and the hard, strong, even-grained wood is widely used to make cabinets, moldings and flooring, and also provides lumber, pilings, poles and pulp. • The crushed needles smell like poison-hemlock (*Conium maculatum*), hence the common name. • In subalpine zones, mountain hemlock (*T. mertensiana*) is distinguishable from western hemlock because its cones are 2–3 times longer and the needles grow in a bottlebrush-like arrangement. **Where found:** moist humid sites along the Coast Ranges; inland along the western and upper eastern slopes of the Cascade Range. **Also known as:** Pacific hemlock, West Coast hemlock, western red hemlock.

# Western White Pine

## *Pinus monticola*

**Height:** up to 130 ft
**Needles:** 2–5 in long, in bundles of 5
**Seed cones:** 4–10 in long, cylindrical, yellow-green to purple (young),
reddish brown and woody (mature)

This lovely large pine is not as abundant in the wild as would be expected because of an introduced fungus that quickly kills young trees. White pine blister rust was brought in by imported eastern white pines. Our native trees are slowing building up a resistance. • Western white pine wood is non-resinous and thus popular for moldings and trim and in handicrafts because it is very soft and workable. The long, distinctive cones are also often used in craftwork. **Where found:** moist valleys to open dry slopes; sea level to subalpine; western Washington and northwestern Oregon; inland coniferous forests throughout the Cascades down to the Siskiyou Mountains.

# Shore Pine

### *Pinus contorta*

**Height:** up to 65 ft
**Needles:** 1–2¾ in long, in pairs
**Cones:** reddish green pollen cones clustered on tips of branches; egg-shaped seed cones 1–2 in long

Shore pine does indeed grow near the shore and does not merely tolerate but seems to thrive in the salty sea spray and ocean winds, making it fairly common along the immediate coast where most other trees can't survive. This tough climate, however, causes this tenacious tree to grow twisted and stunted. • In its non-coastal range, lodgepole pine (*P. contorta* var. *latifolia*) grows straight and tall, to 130 ft. • Native groups used the roots for rope, bark for splints and pitch for waterproofing or as a glue. **Where found:** exposed outer-coastal shorelines, dunes, bogs, rocky hilltops.

# Ponderosa Pine

### *Pinus ponderosa*

**Height:** 33–130 ft
**Needles:** 4–10 in long, in bundles of 3
**Seed cones:** 3–5½ in long

These stately pines thrive in areas that are periodically burned. • The straight, cinnamon-colored trunks are distinctive, with black fissures outlining a jigsaw puzzle of thick plates of bark. • Native peoples ground the oil-rich seeds into meal and collected the sweet inner bark in spring, when the sap was running. Large scars can still be seen on some older trees, attesting to people's fondness for this sweet treat. • The cones have thick, dull brown scales tipped with a stiff prickle. **Where found:** mountains and foothills; east of the Sierra Nevada and Cascade Mountains. **Also known as:** yellow pine.

# Western Yew

### *Taxus brevifolia*

**Height:** 16–33 ft
**Needles:** about ⅝ in long
**Seed cones:** <⅛ in long
**Fruits:** <¼ in across, fleshy, berry-like

This tree's dark, flat evergreen needles and bright scarlet "berries" make it an attractive ornamental and winter forage for wildlife. • The bark contains taxol, a drug used to treat ovarian and breast cancer, and significant overharvesting for this compound has occurred. This species as well as yews in Asia are becoming rare. • The heavy, fine-grained wood is prized by carvers for its purplish red, papery bark over rose-colored inner bark. **Where found:** moist, shady sites in foothills and montane zones; Olympic Peninsula; Coast Range in southern Oregon but rare north of the Umpqua River; scattered localities in the valleys between the Coast and Cascade ranges.

# Western Redcedar

### *Thuja plicata*

**Height:** up to 130 ft
**Needles:** about ⅛ in long
**Seed cones:** ⅜–½ in long

Redcedar has been called the "cornerstone of the northwest coast Indian culture." • The moist inner bark, green buds and oil from the leaves were used medicinally. The inner bark was also stripped, twisted, woven and plaited to make baskets, blankets, mats, clothing and ropes, and sheets of bark and roots were made into containers. Dugout canoes, rafts and frames for birch-bark canoes as well as many other implements were made from the trunks.

Today, this tree's wood is widely used for siding, roofing, paneling, doors, patio furniture, chests and caskets. **Where found:** rich, moist to wet, foothill and montane sites of the Cascades.

# Garry Oak

## *Quercus garryana*

**Height:** 82 ft
**Leaves:** 4¾ in long, deeply lobed
**Flowers:** tiny, inconspicuous catkins
(male) and flower clusters (female)
**Fruit:** edible acorns, ¾–1¼ in long

Roasted acorn kernels taste much like other nuts and can be eaten as a snack, baked in cookies and cakes, or dipped in syrup and eaten like candy. Oak bark teas have been widely used in washes and gargles for treating skin and mouth irritation. Pieces of oak bark were chewed to relieve toothaches, but the tannic acid in this tree is potentially poisonous—cattle and sheep have died from eating oak leaves or large amounts of raw acorns. **Where found:** dry, rocky slopes or bluffs at low elevations. **Also known as:** Oregon white oak.

# Red Alder

## *Alnus rubra*

**Height:** up to 80 ft
**Leaves:** 2–6 in long, broadly elliptical
**Flowers:** hanging catkins; male catkins 2–4¾ in long;
female catkins ¾ in long
**Fruit:** brownish cones, ¾ in long

This tree gets its name from the red color that develops when the bark is scraped or bruised. • A tip for your next fish barbecue: use red alder wood. It is considered the best for smoking fish, especially salmon. It is also an attractive wood for artistic carvings and bowls, and the tannins in the bark can be used for red dye. The bark was used traditionally for a variety of medicinal purposes—reputed to have antibiotic properties, it was used as a tonic and an antibacterial wash. The ancient Romans treated tumors with alder leaves, which modern scientists have since learned contain the tumor-suppressing compounds betulin and lupeol. **Where found:** low-elevation moist woods, streambanks, floodplains, cleared land.

# White Birch

## *Betula papyrifera*

**Height:** 98 ft
**Leaves:** 1⅝–4 in long,
margins double-toothed
**Flowers:** male catkins 2–4 in long,
female catkins ¾–1½ in long
**Fruits:** small, winged nutlets

The smooth, pale bark that peels off in papery sheets was used by Native peoples to make birch-bark canoes. Never peel the bark from a living tree as the tree can be scarred or killed. • Birch wood produces long-burning, sweet-smelling fires (with excellent kindling from the bark) and is extremely hard, making it suitable for making sleds, snowshoes, paddles, canoe ribs, arrows and tool handles. • Betulic acid (the compound that makes birch bark white) is being studied for use in sunscreen and in the treatment of skin cancer. **Where found:** dry to moist sites in foothills to subalpine zones. **Also known as:** paper birch, canoe birch.

# Black Cottonwood

## *Populus balsamifera* ssp. *trichocarpa*

**Height:** up to 160 ft
**Leaves:** 2–6 in
**Flowers:** catkins, male ¾–1¼ in long, female 1⅝–4 in or longer, on separate trees
**Fruit:** oval capsules, ¼ in long, that release fluffy masses of tiny seeds tipped with soft, white hairs

This tree is the largest of the American poplars and largest hardwood in North America. • The young catkins and the sweet inner bark of spring were eaten by many Native groups. Medicinally, the leaves, bark and resins from the sticky, aromatic buds were important for treating many conditions and ailments. Th resins are still used today for salves, cough medicines and painkillers. • The wood is ideal for campfires because it does not crackle and makes clean smoke. **Where found:** moist to wet sites, often on shores, in foothills to subalpine zones. **Also known as:** balsam poplar, balm-of-Gilead, *P. trichocarpa*.

# Quaking Aspen

### *Populus tremuloides*

**Height:** 65–82 ft
**Leaves:** ¾–3 in long
**Flowers:** catkins, ¾–4 in long, male and female catkins on separate trees
**Fruit:** cone-shaped capsules that release many tiny seeds tipped with soft, white hairs

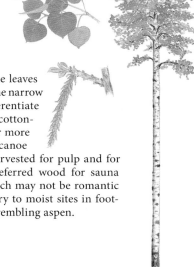

The name "quaking" refers to the way the leaves tremble in the slightest breeze because of the narrow leaf stalks. This is a good way to differentiate quaking aspen from the similar black cotton-wood. • Aspen trunks were once used for more romantic purposes such as tipi poles and canoe paddles; today, the wood is primarily harvested for pulp and for making chopsticks. However, it is a preferred wood for sauna benches because it does not splinter, which may not be romantic but is definitely sensible. **Where found:** dry to moist sites in foot-hills to subalpine zones. **Also known as:** trembling aspen.

# Bitter Cherry

### *Prunus emarginata*

**Height:** 3–50 ft
**Leaves:** 1¼–3 in long, finely toothed, rounded at the tip
**Flowers:** 4–6 in across, white or pinkish, 10–15 in a flat-topped cluster
**Fruit:** red to purple cherries, ⅜ in diameter

The cherries are colorful and juicy, but bite into one and prepare to pucker—the cherries are indeed bitter. They have even been known to cause illness in humans, but animals, especially birds, forage on them. Herbalists, however, claim that bitter cherry essence aids impatience and short attention spans. Native tribes used other parts of the plant for medicinal purposes, such as poultices and bark infusions and used long, fibrous strips of bark for twine and basketry. **Where found:** rocky slopes, canyons, chaparral, mixed forest, moist forest, along streams at low to mid elevations; pioneer species on logged sites.

# Pacific Madrone

## *Arbutus menziesii*

**Height:** 50–100 ft
**Leaves:** 2–6 in long
**Flowers:** ¼ in long, greenish white, sweet fragrance
**Fruit:** ¼ in long, pea-sized, persists on tree into winter

The Latin *Arbutus* and Spanish *madrone* translate to "strawberry tree," referring to the red fruits. • These trees are drought tolerant and are excellent cliff stabilizers because their long roots reach as far as the bedrock in search of water. • Medicinally, Pacific madrone was used traditionally to treat colds, stomach problems, as an astringent, as a tea to treat bladder infections, in sitz baths for other types of infections and as a postpartum contraceptive. **Where found:** canyon and mountain slopes from sea level to 5000 ft.

# Pacific Dogwood

## *Cornus nuttallii*

**Height:** 65 ft
**Leaves:** 3–4 in
**Flowers:** tiny, greenish purple–tipped, in clusters surrounded by 4–6 showy, white or pinkish 2–5 in bracts
**Fruit:** red berries, <½ in across, in clusters

When in flower in early spring, Pacific dogwood adds an exotic flair to the dull periphery of coniferous forests, flirting with the stately pines, spruce and Douglas-fir. In autumn, the leaves turn a delicate pinkish red. • This tree is becoming rare in the Pacific Northwest owing to its susceptibility to a fungal disease called anthracnose. **Where found:** moist, well-drained sites, such as along streambeds, in low-elevation mixed forests up to 1500 ft, on western Cascade slopes.

# Bigleaf Maple

### *Acer macrophyllum*

**Height:** 115 ft
**Leaves:** 6–12 in across, 5-lobed
**Flowers:** ⅛ in across, greenish yellow, numerous, in hanging clusters
**Fruit:** paired samaras, 1–2⅜ in long, wings in a V-shape

Moss thrives on the bigleaf maple with such exuberance that the bark is often completely enrobed. The moss forms a thick layer in the tree's canopy, creating a "floating soil" onto which other plants sprout and root. Vine maple (*A. circinatum*), another common maple in our area, also produces this canopy effect. • The maples of the West do not produce either the quantity or the sweetness of the famed maple syrup of their eastern counterparts. **Where found:** dry to moist sites, often with Douglas-fir; often on sites disturbed by fire, clearing or logging; low to mid elevations. **Also known as:** Oregon maple.

# Oregon Ash

### *Fraxinus latifolia*

**Height:** 80 ft
**Leaves:** compound, 5–7 leaflets, each 5 in long
**Flowers:** ⅛ in wide, inconspicuous
**Fruit:** samaras, 1¼–2 in long, in dense clusters

Oregon ash is the only native *Fraxinus* species in the Pacific Northwest. It is a member of the olive family (Oleaceae). • Deer and elk browse on this plant, and it makes good firewood. It is also a popular ornamental and can be found in gardens and lining city streets. • This tree may reach 250 years of age and grows quickly in its youth but growth slows with age. **Where found:** moist to wet soils at low elevations; near streams and along the Columbia River; shores of Puget Sound; from the coast into the western Cascade Range and along the southwestern coast, but not in Olympic Mountains; prominent in valleys, particularly the Willamette Valley.

# SHRUBS

Shrubs survive several seasons and are therefore perennials. They have one or more woody stems or can be a vine, and they are normally less than 16 ft tall. Shrubs may produce flowers and fruit. They provide habitat and shelter for a variety of animals, and their berries, leaves and often bark are crucial sources of food. The tasty berries of some shrubs have been a staple of native and traditional foods, and they are still enjoyed by people everywhere.

Juniper
p. 169

Prince's-pine
p. 169

Falsebox
p. 169

Heath Family
pp. 170–72

Oregon-grape
p. 172

Willow
p. 172

Dogwood
p. 173

Rose Family
pp. 173–75

Scotch Broom
p. 176

Sagebrush & Rabbitbrush
p. 176

Buckthorns
p. 177

Currants
pp. 177–78

Honeysuckles
pp. 178–79

Poison Oak
p. 179

# Common Juniper

### *Juniperus communis*

**Height:** 1–3½ ft
**Needles:** ¼–¾ in long, sometimes scale-like
**Seed cones:** about ½ in long

Blue-gray juniper "berries" are, in fact, tiny cones with fleshy scales. They can add spice to food and flavoring to gin, but pregnant women and people with kidney problems should never use them, and they can be toxic in large quantities. • Europeans made juniper berry tea to treat eating disorders, diarrhea and heart, lung, and kidney problems. Native peoples burned juniper branches of this pungently aromatic evergreen to purify homes, protect people from evil and bring good luck to hunters. **Where found:** dry, open sites in plains to alpine zones.

# Prince's-pine

### *Chimaphila umbellata*

**Height:** 4–12 in
**Leaves:** ¾–3 in, whorled, evergreen
**Flowers:** <½ in long, pink, waxy
**Fruit:** round capsules, ¼ in across

Prince's-pine has been used to flavor candy, soft drinks (especially root beer) and traditional beers. The leaves of this semi-woody, evergreen shrub are glossy and dark green above and pale beneath. The flowers are waxy. • Native peoples used a tea made from this plant as a remedy for fluid retention, kidney or bladder problems, fevers and coughs. Several Native groups smoked the dried leaves. • These attractive plants need certain soil fungi to live, so they usually die when transplanted. They are best enjoyed in the wild. **Where found:** wooded (usually coniferous) foothills and montane zones. **Also known as:** pipsissewa.

# Falsebox

### *Paxistima myrsinites*

**Height:** 8–24 in
**Leaves:** ½–1¼ in long, leathery, shiny
**Flowers:** ⅛ in wide, maroon, in small clusters
**Fruit:** oval capsules, ⅛ in long

The glossy, stiff, leathery leaves of these low, branched, evergreen shrubs blanket the floor of many mountain forests. Sprays of falsebox are often used in flower arrangements, and over-collecting has depleted many populations. • The greenish brown to dark reddish flowers are borne in small clusters in the leaf axils. • To remember this plant's unusual scientific name, just repeat "Pa kissed ma." **Where found:** moist forests to well-drained, open sites in foothills and montane and subalpine zones. **Also known as:** mountain boxwood, *Pachistima myrsinites*.

# Common Bearberry

### *Arctostaphylos uva-ursi*

**Height:** 2–6 in
**Leaves:** ½–1¼ in long, leathery
**Flowers:** ⅛–¼ in long, pinkish white, urn-shaped
**Fruit:** berry-like drupes, ¼–½ in across, bright red

Thick, leathery evergreen leaves help this common, mat-forming shrub to survive on dry, sunny slopes where others would perish. • The "berries" are edible, but rather mealy and tasteless. Native groups cooked them and mixed them with grease or fish eggs to reduce their dryness. The glossy leaves were widely used for smoking, both alone and later with tobacco. • The long, trailing branches send down roots, and the flowers nod in small clusters. **Where found:** well-drained, open or wooded sites in foothills to alpine zones; western and northeastern Oregon north through Washington. **Also known as:** kinnikinnick.

# Salal

### *Gaultheria shallon*

**Height:** 1–4 ft average, up to 7 ft
**Leaves:** 2–4 in long, leathery, glossy
**Flowers:** ¼ in across, pink to white, in clusters
**Fruit:** bluish black, edible berry, ¼ in across

The edible berries of salal were an important food source to Native peoples, but they are mealy and were typically dried or mixed with animal fat or fish oil or eggs. A tea made from the leaves was used to treat several ailments, or the leaves were dried along with *Arctostaphylos* leaves and smoked like tobacco. **Where found:** warm, dry, well-drained sites, tolerant of salt spray, rocky soil; from the west slope of the Cascades to the coast; conifer forests from sea level to montane zones.

# Black Huckleberry

### *Vaccinium membranaceum*

**Height:** 1–5 ft
**Leaves:** ¾–2 in long
**Flowers:** ¼ in long, creamy pink to yellow-pink
**Fruit:** blue-black berries, ¼–½ in across

Black huckleberries are among our most delicious and highly prized berries. They are plentiful in open, subalpine sites such as old burns, and in some areas, they are sold commercially. Native peoples ate them fresh, sun-dried or smoke-dried for winter use (either loose or mashed and formed into cakes). Today, huckleberries are made into jams and jellies, or used in pancakes, muffins and desserts. • The finely toothed, deciduous leaves turn red or purple in autumn. **Where found:** moist, open sites in foothills and montane zones. **Also known as:** *V. globulare*.

# Grouseberry

### *Vaccinium scoparium*

**Height:** 4–8 in
**Leaves:** ¼–½ in long
**Flowers:** ⅛ in long, pink, bell-shaped, nodding, solitary
**Fruit:** round berries, bright red to purplish, ⅛–¼ in across

It could take hours to collect even a small quantity of
these tiny, sweet berries, but some Native peoples gathered
them using combs. Many birds, particularly grouse, and small
mammals enjoy many parts of this small deciduous shrub. The
dense leafy, broom-like branches often form lacy mats. • Another *Vaccinium*,
evergreen huckleberry (*V. ovatum*), is abundant close to the ocean and in the
Olympics and stays green year round. **Where found:** open or wooded sites; foothills, montane and subalpine zones. **Also known as:** whortleberry.

# False Azalea

### *Menziesia ferruginea*

**Height:** 1½–6½ ft
**Leaves:** 1¼–2½ in long, in clusters along branches
**Flowers:** about ¼ in long, pinkish to yellowish white, urn-shaped
**Fruit:** oval capsules, ¼ in long

This deciduous shrub is sometimes called "fool's huckleberry," because it looks like a huckleberry, but its fruit is
a dry capsule, not a berry. • Like many members of the heath family
(Ericaceae), this plant contains the poison andromedotoxin. • The
sticky-hairy twigs of false azalea smell skunky when crushed. The thin, dull, pale
green, glandular-hairy leaves are mostly clustered near branch tips and turn
crimson in fall. **Where found:** moist woods in foothills and montane zones. **Also
known as:** fool's huckleberry, *M. glabella*.

# Pacific Rhododendron

### *Rhododendron macrophyllum*

**Height:** average 10 ft, up to 20 ft
**Leaves:** evergreen, 7 in long, leathery
**Flowers:** ¾–1½ in long, pink, bell-shaped, 15–20 in terminal clusters
**Fruit:** woody capsules, ¼ in long

In spring, mountainsides blush with pink blooms and the understories
of coniferous forests are brightened with this colorful species. The range of
this wild rhododendron is reduced where populations struggle in the wild
against those who poach it for their gardens. • Rhododendrons are very poisonous
plants, containing a neurotoxin called grayanotoxin. Though wild animals are wary,
livestock is often careless, and this plant has to be cleared from grazing lands.
• This lovely flower has been the Washington state flower since 1892. **Where found:**
moist to fairly dry coniferous or mixed forests; coast to mid-elevation mountains.

171

# Pink Mountain-heather

### *Phyllodoce empetriformis*

**Height:** to 12 ft
**Leaves:** ³⁄₈ in long
**Flowers:** ¼ in long, bell-shaped, erect to nodding
**Fruit:** round capsules, ⅛ in across

When this evergreen comes into bloom, the rose-pink clusters of tiny bells announce spring in the mountains, delighting hikers, and can set several acres ablush. The needle-like leaves help these ground-hugging plants to survive in areas where frozen soil and cold, dry winds limit water. It is not a true heather but is very similar in appearance to its European cousin (*Calluna* spp.). • Although this plant grows in alpine regions, Phyllodoce was a sea-nymph in Greek mythology. **Where found:** subalpine and alpine elevations; Olympic Mountains and northern Cascades. **Also known as:** red heather, red mountain-heather.

# Tall Oregon-grape

### *Berberis aquifolium*

**Height:** 6 ft
**Leaves:** 6–12 in long, divided into 5–9 spiny leaflets, each 2–3 in long
**Flowers:** tiny, yellow, bell-shaped, in clusters 1–2½ in across
**Fruit:** bluish berry, <½ in across

In 1899, Oregon-grape was declared the Oregon state flower. • These evergreens are popular in gardens, and their reddish, holly-like winter leaves make them attractive as Christmas decorations. • The juicy grape-like berries are sour but can be eaten raw, make good jam and wine and are sometimes mixed with salal berries to make jelly. • Herbalists make a tincture from the bright yellow roots to treat digestion problems. **Where found:** exposed areas and dry, rocky sites in foothills and on montane slopes. **Also known as:** *Mahonia aquifolium.*

# Scouler's Willow

### *Salix scouleriana*

**Height:** 6½–30 ft
**Leaves:** 1¼–4 in long
**Catkins:** ³⁄₄–1⁵⁄₈ in long
**Fruit:** silky capsules, ¼–³⁄₈ in long

Willows are extremely common, but it is often difficult to identify each species. Dense, elongating flower clusters (catkins) and buds covered by a single scale identify this group. • Scouler's willow is a spindly, clumped, deciduous shrub with short, stiff, rust-colored hairs on the undersides of its leaves. The seed (female) catkins appear before the leaves and produce long-beaked, short-stalked, hairy capsules containing tiny, silky-tufted seeds. • Sitka willow (*S. sitchensis*) grow 3–26 ft tall, with brittle twigs, silky capsules and catkins 2–3 in long that often appear before the leaves in spring. **Where found:** moist to wet sites in foothills and montane zones; western in range.

# Red-osier Dogwood

### *Cornus sericea*

**Height:** 1½–10 ft
**Leaves:** ¾–4 in long, prominently veined
**Flowers:** <¼ in wide, white, in dense clusters
**Fruit:** berry-like drupes, about ¼ in wide

This attractive, hardy, deciduous shrub has distinctive purple to red branches with white flowers in spring, red leaves in autumn and white "berries" in winter. It is easily grown from cuttings. • Native peoples smoked the dried inner bark alone or with tobacco or common bearberry (kinnikinnick). The flexible branches were often woven into baskets, especially as decorative red rims. The bitter, juicy berries, mixed with sweeter fruit or sugar, made "sweet-and-sour." **Where found:** moist sites in plains, foothills and montane zones. **Also known as:** *C. stolonifera.*

# Saskatoon

### *Amelanchier alnifolia*

**Height:** 3½–12 ft
**Leaves:** ¾–2 in long, top half regularly toothed
**Flowers:** ¾ in wide, white, 5 petals
**Fruit:** purple-black, berry-like pomes, ¼–½ in across

Many Native groups gathered these sweet, juicy "berries." Large quantities were dried (loose or in cakes) and mixed with meat and fat, or added to stews. Today, the berries are used in pies, pancakes, muffins, jams, jellies, syrups and wine. These hardy, deciduous shrubs are easily propagated. They have beautiful blossoms in spring, delicious fruit in summer and scarlet leaves in autumn. **Where found:** dry, rocky areas; widespread west of the Cascades below 2000 ft; more abundant in the northeast. **Also known as:** juneberry, serviceberry.

# Western Mountain-ash

### *Sorbus scopulina*

**Height:** 3½–13 ft
**Leaves:** compound, leaflets 1¼–2½ in long
**Flowers:** <½ in wide, white, in large, dense, flat-topped clusters
**Fruit:** reddish orange pomes, ¼–⅜ in across, in clusters

Deep green, glossy leaves and showy clusters of white flowers or glossy "berries" make western mountain-ash an attractive deciduous shrub. The juicy berries also provide food for many birds. Some Native peoples ate these bitter fruits fresh or dried, but many considered them inedible. Today, they are sometimes made into jams and jellies. **Where found:** moist sites in foothills and montane and subalpine zones.

# Thimbleberry

### *Rubus parviflorus*

**Height:** 1½–6½ ft
**Leaves:** 2–8 in wide, 3–7-lobed, similar to a maple leaf
**Flowers:** 1–2 in wide, white
**Fruit:** raspberry-like, red, ⅝–¾ in wide

These beautiful, satiny berries are seedy and difficult to collect, but most Native peoples ate them fresh from the bush because they are so common. Thimbleberries can be tasteless, tart or sweet, depending on the season and the site, but birds and bears always seem to enjoy them. • Native peoples also ate the young shoots, and the broad, 2–8 in wide leaves provided temporary plates, containers and basket liners. • This deciduous shrub, without prickles, often forms dense thickets. **Where found:** moist to dry sites in foothills and montane zones.

# Ninebark

### *Physocarpus capitatus*

**Height:** 12 ft
**Leaves:** 1½–3½ in wide, 1⅛–2⅜ in long, 3–5-lobed
**Flowers:** ½ in long, white, 5 petals, in rounded clusters
**Fruit:** reddish brown follicles, ¼ in long, in dense, upright clusters

Although it is slightly toxic, many Native groups used this plant medicinally, following the old adage that "what doesn't kill you, cures you." • This shrub is named for the supposedly 9 layers of bark that can be peeled away from the stem. • The leaves turn to intense reds and oranges in fall. **Where found:** wet, somewhat open places such as in thickets along streams and lakes, coastal marshes and edges of moist woodlands; low to mid elevation Cascades.

# Birch-leaved Spiraea

### *Spiraea betulifolia*

**Height:** 16–28 in
**Leaves:** ¾–2¾ in long
**Flowers:** <¼ in across, white to purplish, in clusters 1¼–3 in wide
**Fruit:** pod-like capsules, ⅛ in across, joined at the base in clusters of 5

These attractive deciduous shrubs are easily overlooked, but when they bloom, their showy flower clusters catch the eyes of passersby. • Birch-leaved spiraea is hardy and easily grown from cuttings, shoots or seeds, but once established, it spreads rapidly by rhizomes, and can become difficult to control. • Grouse eat the young leaves, and deer also browse on these shrubs. **Where found:** dry, open forests; bunchgrass and Ponderosa pine ecosystems; low to mid elevations east of the Cascades. **Also known as:** *S. lucida.*

# Oceanspray

### *Holodiscus discolor*

**Height:** up to 10 ft
**Leaves:** ¾–2½ in long, hairy
**Flowers:** tiny, creamy white, in hanging clusters 4–7 in long
**Fruit:** tiny, light brown, in large clusters that persist through winter

As its name attests, this species is very tolerant of salt spray and maritime conditions, though it is also common inland on the western slopes of the Cascade Mountains. Its hardiness makes it a pioneer species on disturbed sites. • Imaginative minds have drawn comparison between the drooping clusters of tiny white flowers and frothy sea foam dripping from the shrubs hanging over coastal cliffsides. **Where found:** coast to low montane forest edges and cliffsides of the western Cascade slopes. **Also known as:** creambush.

# Shrubby Cinquefoil

### *Dasiphora floribunda*

**Height:** 1–4 ft
**Leaves:** compound, leaflets ½–¾ in long, grayish green
**Flowers:** ¾ in, yellow, 5 petals
**Fruit:** achenes ⅝–1¼ in wide, light brown, hairy

This hardy, deciduous shrub is sometimes also seen in gardens and public places. It is often covered with bright yellow blooms from spring to fall. Shrubby cinquefoil also provides erosion control, especially along highways. • Heavily browsed cinquefoils indicate overgrazing, as most animals prefer other plants. • Native peoples used the papery, shredding bark as tinder for fires. **Where found:** wet to dry, often rocky sites from plains to subalpine zones. **Also known as:** *Potentilla fruticosa, Pentaphylloides floribunda.*

# Bitterbrush

### *Purshia tridentata*

**Height:** to 8 ft
**Leaves:** 1 in long
**Flowers:** ⅝ in long, yellow, tubular, solitary
**Fruit:** about ⅝ in long, spindle-shaped, seed-like

Bitterbrush has very similar leaves to sagebrush (though they are not aromatic), but it has small, rose-like flowers and velvety, seed-like fruits. It is an abundant shrub and an important member of the sagebrush community and dry parts of the state. Its hardiness and abundance makes this plant important forage for deer and elk, and the abundant yellow flowers add splashes of color to the dry landscape. **Where found:** abundant in dry areas, along interior roads; sagebrush and bunchgrass ecosystems; central and southeastern Washington, south through Oregon. **Also known as:** antelopebrush.

# Scotch Broom

### *Cytisus scoparius*

**Height:** 6–8 ft
**Leaves:** ½–1 in long, divided into 3 leaflets
**Flowers:** ¾–1 in long, yellow
**Fruit:** flattened, black pods, 1–1½ in long

Bright masses of golden-yellow flowers fill hedges, ditches and roadsides with radiant color, though it is not regarded with much pleasure by botanists. This shrub is classified as a noxious weed. An invasive, introduced species from Europe, it is amazingly prolific and spreads rapidly over wide areas. Reportedly, only 3 seeds planted on Vancouver Island, Canada, in 1850, subsequently colonized the entire island. **Where found:** low elevations; open and disturbed sites; invading natural meadows and open forests.

# Big Sagebrush

### *Artemisia tridentata*

**Height:** 1½–6½ ft
**Leaves:** ½–¾ in long, silvery, 3 teeth at the tip
**Flowers:** very small, yellow, in heads ½–2¾ in wide
**Fruit:** achenes

This plant is not a true sage family, but rather a species of aster. • These common shrubs, with a pungent, sage-like aroma and grayish, shredding bark, have been used in a wide variety of medicines and were also burned as smudges and fumigants. • Big sagebrush is a valuable food for many wild birds and mammals, but livestock avoid it. Early settlers knew that its presence indicated groundwater. **Where found:** often covering many acres of dry plains and slopes; central and southeastern Washington into and throughout central Oregon.

# Rabbitbush

### *Ericameria nauseosa*

**Height:** 8–24 in
**Leaves:** 1¼–2½ in long, narrow, gray-green, velvety
**Flowers:** ¼ in wide, yellow, in dense clusters
**Fruit:** tufted achenes

In late summer, these flat-topped, deciduous shrubs cover dry slopes with splashes of yellow. A hardy species, this plant thrives on poor soils and in harsh conditions. • Native peoples made medicinal teas from the roots or leaves to treat coughs, colds, fevers and menstrual pain. The dense branches were used to cover and carpet sweathouses, and they were burned slowly to smoke hides. Boiled flowerheads produced a lemon yellow dye for wool, leather and baskets. **Where found:** dry, open areas on plains, foothills and in montane zones in eastern Washington. **Also known as:** rubber rabbitbush, *Chrysothamnus nauseosus*.

# Deerbrush

### *Ceanothus integerrimus*

**Height:** 4–8 ft
**Leaves:** to 2 in long, glossy
**Flowers:** tiny, white or blue, in plumes 2–6 in long
**Fruit:** dry capsules, each with a hard seed

Though this shrub has individuals with white flowers and others have light blue or even dark blue flowers, they are all the same species of *Ceanothus*. • Deerbrush is found in association with the sagebrush community of hardy shrubs. • These shrubs are important forage for deer and other ungulates such as elk. **Where found:** Cascade Range.

# Cascara Buckthorn

### *Rhamnus purshiana*

**Height:** 16–32 ft
**Leaves:** 2–6 in long, oval, dark, shiny
**Flowers:** ⅛ in long, greenish yellow, 5 petals
**Fruit:** berry, ¼ in across, bright red maturing to deep purple or black

Cascara is the largest buckthorn species. • The bark was used as a natural laxative by both Native groups and settlers, and in natural medicine in modern times. The edible fruit does not have laxative properties but is not very tasty. **Where found:** moist, acidic soils in shady clearings or in the under-story of forest edges; mixed forests; low to mid elevations; Coast and Sierra Nevada ranges north. **Also known as:** Pursh's buckthorn; commercially called "cascara sagrada"; in olden times called "chitticum bark."

# Squaw Currant

### *Ribes cereum*

**Height:** 1½–5 ft
**Leaves:** ¼–1 in long, ⅜–1⅝ in wide, 3–5-lobed
**Flowers:** <⅜ in long, white to pink, tubular, in drooping clusters
**Fruit:** red berries, ¼ in wide

These tasteless to bitter, glandular berries (currants) were eaten only occasionally by Native peoples. Some considered them a tonic, whereas others ate them to relieve diarrhea. • The usually sticky-hairy, tubular flowers hang in clusters of 1–8 and are an important source of nectar for hummingbirds early in the year. • The species name *cereum* means "waxy," in reference to the waxy appearance of the glandular, often sticky-hairy leaves. **Where found:** dry sites on plains, foothills and montane slopes east of the Cascades. **Also known as:** wax currant.

# Bristly Black Currant

### *Ribes lacustre*

**Height:** 1½–5 ft
**Leaves:** 1¼–1⅝ in wide, usually 5-lobed
**Flowers:** ¼ in wide, reddish to maroon, in clusters
**Fruit:** dark purple berries, ¼–⅜ in across

Many Native groups ate these edible but insipid berries, fresh or cooked. Today, bristly black currants are usually made into jam. The branch spines of this deciduous shrub cause serious allergic reactions in sensitive people, and some consider the branches (and by extension, the bristly, glandular fruit) to be poisonous. • Wild currants are the intermediate host for blister rust, a virulent disease of native 5-needled pines. • The small flowers are reddish to maroon, hanging in clusters of 7–15. **Where found:** moist, wooded or open sites in foothills to alpine zones.

# Common Snowberry

### *Symphoricarpos albus*

**Height:** 1½–2½ ft
**Leaves:** ¾–1⅝ in long
**Flowers:** ⅛–¼ in long, pink to white, bell-shaped, in clusters
**Fruit:** white, berry-like drupes, ¼–½ in across, in clusters

The name "snowberry" refers to the waxy, white "berries" that remain in small clusters near branch tips through winter. All parts of this deciduous shrub are toxic, causing vomiting and diarrhea. Some Native groups called the fruits "corpse berries" because they were believed to be part of the spirit world, not to be eaten by the living. • The broadly funnel-shaped flowers are pink to white and have hairy centers. **Where found:** well-drained sites from the plains to lower subalpine zones.

# Twinberry

### *Lonicera involucrata*

**Height:** 3½–6½ ft
**Leaves:** 2–6 in long
**Flowers:** ½–¾ in long, yellow, tubular
**Fruit:** black berries, <⅜ in across, in pairs

The unusual, shiny berries of these deciduous shrubs, with their broad, spreading, backward-bending, shiny red to purplish bracts, catch the eyes of passersby and also of hungry bears and birds. Despite their tempting appearance, these berries are unpalatable, and they can be toxic. **Where found:** moist to wet, usually shaded sites in foothills and montane and subalpine zones throughout the Olympic and Cascade mountains. **Also known as:** bracted honeysuckle.

# Black Elderberry

### *Sambucus racemosa* var. *melanocarpa*

**Height:** 3½–10 ft
**Leaves:** compound, 5–7 leaflets, each 2–6 in long
**Flowers:** ⅛–¼ in wide, whitish, in clusters
**Fruit:** black, berry-like drupes, <¼ in across

Large, showy clusters of flowers or heavy, wide "berries" draw attention to this strong-smelling, clumped, deciduous shrub. The berries can be made into jam, jelly, pies and wine, but they are unpalatable and even toxic when raw or immature. The rest of the plant is poisonous to humans, though moose, deer and elk seem to enjoy it. **Where found:** moist sites in foothills and montane and subalpine zones.

# Poison Oak

### *Toxicodendron diversilobum*

**Height:** 3–7 ft, sometimes vining up to 50 ft
**Leaves:** 3–5 irregular lobes (similar to an oak leaf), 1–2 in long
**Flowers:** tiny, yellow, 5 petals, in loose racemes
**Fruit:** berries, ¼ in across, white or cream-colored

Poison oak is not an oak, and poison ivy is not an ivy, but both are members of the sumac family (Anacardiaceae) and both contain the potent allergen urushiol. This substance can stay active on unwashed clothing or on cut branches for up to a year, and smoke from burning branches can damage lung, nose and throat tissues. Not everyone is affected, but some people contract a painful, red, long-lasting rash. Avoid this plant by remembering the rhyme "Leaves of three, let it be." • The leaves turn bright scarlet in autumn. **Where found:** sea level to 5000 ft.

# HERBS, FERNS & SEAWEEDS

The plants in this section are all non-woody plants and include herbs, ferns and seaweeds. Herbs and ferns can be annual, though many are perennial, growing from a persistent rootstock. Most of those with flowering stems later produce fruit. Various forms of seeds are familiar, such as those of the sunflower, a favored treat, and the dandelion, whose white parachuted seeds are irresistible fun to blow into the wind. Many of these plants can be used for adding flavor to foods, and in medicine, aromatherapy and dyes. The many different and unique flowers give us pleasure for their delicate and often breathtaking beauty in color and form. They are the inspiration of artists and poets and are often symbols of romance, or have meanings attached to them through folklore, legend or superstition.

Seaweeds are algae and can be classified into 3 major groups: green, red and brown. They absorb all the required fluids, nutrients and gases directly from the water and, unlike terrestrial plants, do not require an inner system for conducting fluids and nutrients. However, seaweeds do contain chlorophyll to absorb the sunlight needed for photosynthesis. They also contain other light-absorbing pigments, which give some seaweeds their red or brown coloration. Instead of roots, seaweeds have "holdfasts" to anchor them to the sea floor. Many seaweeds have hollow, gas-filled floats, which help to keep the photosynthetic structures of these organisms buoyant and close to the water's surface so that they can absorb sunlight. Seaweeds provide food and shelter for marine animals, and dense, underwater seaweed "forests" are an important part of many marine ecosystems. Seaweeds also provide food for humans in some cultures and have a variety of medicinal and industrial uses as well.

**Lilies**
pp. 182–84

**Skunk Cabbage**
p. 184

**Purslanes**
p. 185

**Chickweed & Catchfly**
p. 186

**Mustard Family**
pp. 186–87

**Poppy & Bleeding Heart**
p. 188

**Saxifrages & Sedum**
pp. 188–89

**Buttercup Family**
pp. 190–91

**Strawberry**
p. 191

**Sorrel**
p. 192

**Violet**
p. 192

**Pea Family**
pp. 192–93

**Fireweed**
p. 193

**Cow Parsnip**
p. 194

**Gentian**
p. 194

**Waterleaf Family**
pp. 194–95

**Phlox**
p. 195

**Pennyroyal**
p. 196

**Bedstraw**
p. 196

**Snapdragons**
pp. 196–98

**Aster Family**
pp. 198–200

**Valerian**
p. 200

**Ferns**
p. 201

**Seaweeds & Algae**
pp. 202–03

# Nodding Onion

### *Allium cernuum*

**Height:** 4–12 in
**Leaves:** 1/8–1/4 in wide, basal, grass-like
**Flowers:** 1/4 in wide, pink to purplish, bell-shaped, nodding
**Fruit:** 1/8 in long, 3 lobed capsules (bulbs), 1/2–3/4 in thick

When they are not in flower, wild onions are distinguished from their poisonous relative, meadow death camas, by their strong onion smell. Do not try the taste test. • Many Native groups enjoyed wild onions as a vegetable and as flavoring in other foods. Cooking decreases the strong odor and makes the bulbs sweeter and easier to digest. Bears, ground squirrels and marmots also enjoy wild onions. **Where found:** moist to dry, open sites in plains, foothills and montane zones.

# Corn Lily

### *Clintonia uniflora*

**Height:** 2½–6 in
**Leaves:** 3–6 in long, 1¼–2 in wide, basal
**Flowers:** 3/4–1 in wide, solitary
**Fruit:** single berry, 3/8–1/2 in wide

This common woodland wildflower brightens the forest floor in spring and early summer. The 2–4 slightly fleshy, glossy basal leaves have hairy edges. • Although the bright metallic blue berries are unpalatable by human standards, grouse seem to enjoy them. • This native perennial can live for 30 or more years. **Where found:** moist to wet, montane and subalpine forests and clearings. **Also known as:** clintonia, bride's bonnet, queen's cup.

# Chocolate Lily

### *Fritillaria lanceolata*

**Height:** 30 in
**Leaves:** 2–6 in long, 1–2 whorls of 3–5
**Flowers:** nodding bells, 1½ in long, single or in clusters of 2–5
**Fruit:** upright, 6-angled capsules with wings

The bulbs of this lily are edible and were eaten by coastal Native groups. They boiled the bulbs as well as the "bulblets," which are said to be similar to rice, though bitter. • Today, this flower is very rare and should be left undisturbed—and uneaten. **Where found:** grassy meadows, open woods; sea level to nearly subalpine; along the coast and inland along major drainages. **Also known as:** checker lily, mission bells, *F. affinis*.

# False Lily-of-the-valley

### *Maianthemum dilatatum*

**Height:** 4–15¾ in
**Leaves:** 1–3, alternate, heart-shaped, up to 4 in long
**Flowers:** tiny, with parts in 4s, in terminal cylindrical clusters
**Fruit:** round berries, ¼ in across, light green to brown, maturing to red

Inspiring myths throughout recorded time, the flowers of this plant supposedly grew from the tears of the Virgin and the blood of Christian saints. They were regarded as sacred to the goddess Maia and the god Hermes and thus were significant in alchemy and astrology. • In Haida myth, the berries were part of a feast for supernatural beings. **Where found:** moist to wet, usually shady woods, riverside areas; groundcover of Sitka spruce forests near the coast; low to mid elevations; common on the Olympic Peninsula. **Also known as:** maianthemum, deerberry, snakeberry, mayflower, may lily, two-leaved Solomon's-seal, wild lily-of-the-valley.

# Star-flowered False Solomon's-seal

### *Maianthemum stellatum*

**Height:** ½–2 ft
**Leaves:** 1¼–4¾ in long
**Flowers:** <½ in wide
**Fruit:** berries, ¼–½ in across

The species name *stellata*, from the Latin *stella*, "star," aptly describes the radiant, white blossoms of this woodland wildflower. • This unbranched, slightly arching plant produces clusters of dark blue or reddish black berries, which are greenish yellow with purplish stripes when young. • A larger relative, false Solomon's-seal (*M. racemosum*) is easily recognized by its 2–6 in long, puffy, pyramidal flower clusters and its wavy (rather than straight-edged) leaves. **Where found:** moist to dry sites in foothills to subalpine zones. **Also known as:** *Smilacina stellata*.

# Wake Robin

### *Trillium ovatum*

**Height:** 4–16 in
**Leaves:** 2–6 in long, in whorls of 3
**Flowers:** 2½–3½ in across, white
**Fruit:** berry-like capsules, green, slightly winged

This wildflower is one of the first showy blooms to grace the forest each spring. • Trillium, from the Latin *tri*, "three," refers to the 3 leaves, 3 petals, 3 sepals and 3 stigmas. • Each seed has a small, oil-rich body that attracts ants. The ants carry seeds to their nests, eat the oil-rich part and discard the rest, thus dispersing and planting new trilliums. • The fruits are numerous yellowish green, berry-like capsules, which are shed in a sticky mass. **Where found:** moist to wet, shady sites from foothills to subalpine zones. **Also known as:** western trillium, Pacific trillium.

# Green False-Hellebore

### *Veratrum viride*

**Height:** 2½–6½ ft
**Leaves:** 4–14 in long, prominently ribbed
**Flowers:** ¾ in across, star-shaped, pale green, numerous
**Fruit:** brown, oblong capsules, ¾–1¼ in long

The lush, accordion-pleated leaves of green false-hellebore appear soon after snowmelt. By midsummer, waist-high plants produce hundreds of musky-smelling flowers in long, nodding tassels. • All parts of this plant are deadly poisonous and it is one of the most poisonous in Pacific Northwest forests. Dried plants have been used as a garden insecticide, and water from boiled roots was used to kill lice. **Where found:** moist to wet, open sites in montane to subalpine zones. **Also known as:** Indian hellebore, corn lily, *V. eschscholtzii.*

# Meadow Death Camas

### *Zigadenus venenosus*

**Height:** 18–23 in
**Leaves:** up to 12 in long
**Flowers:** tiny, white, saucer-shaped, in a terminal cluster 6–8 in long
**Fruit:** 3-lobed capsules, ¾ in long

Deadly poisonous, the bulbs of this plant are very similar in appearance to those of the blue-flowered edible camas (*Camassia* spp.), or quamash, which was an important food staple to Native groups and which often grows alongside death camas. The edible variety is easily identifiable by the flowers (purple vs. white). • This plant is notorious for poisoning sheep and occasionally other livestock, but well-fed animals usually avoid it. • The toxic alkaloids cause tingling upon contact to the mouth, but ingestion results in convulsions, coma, and then death. **Where found:** wet areas, open forests or forest edges, rocky or grassy slopes; low to mid elevations.

# Skunk Cabbage

### *Lysichiton americanum*

**Height:** 1–5 ft
**Leaves:** 40–60 in long, 20 in wide, in a large, basal rosette
**Flowers:** tiny, greenish yellow, in a spike up to 14 in tall
**Fruit:** berry-like, pulpy, green-yellow

Skunk cabbage belongs to the large and worldwide arum family (Araceae). • The complex inflorescence consists of an encircling yellow spathe and a central columnar spadix packed with hundreds of tiny, yellowish flowers. The flower emits a strong, skunky scent that attracts small beetles to pollinate it. • Native peoples used the large leaves for packaging, lining berry baskets and serving food, lending it the nickname "Indian wax paper." • Grizzly bears eat skunk cabbage, so hikers beware. **Where found:** moist or wet sites, marshes, bogs, swamps; low and mid elevations; near coastal conifer forests.

# Lanceleaf Springbeauty

### *Claytonia lanceolata*

**Height:** 2–4 in
**Leaves:** ⅝–2½ in long, stem leaves opposite
**Flowers:** ½–⅝ in wide, white or pale pink
**Fruit:** egg-shaped capsules, ⅛ in long

These delicate, fleshy perennials are often found hugging the ground near late snow patches at high elevations. • The leaves are edible, and the corms are said to taste like mild radishes when raw and like potatoes when cooked. Native peoples collected the deep-growing, small, wide, corms in spring, as the white to pinkish blossoms faded. **Where found:** moist, open sites in foothills to alpine zones. **Also known as:** western springbeauty.

# Miner's Lettuce

### *Claytonia perfoliata*

**Height:** 1–16 in
**Leaves:** up to 4 in wide, 2 stem leaves usually fused into a disk
**Flowers:** ⅛–¼ in wide, numerous (5–40), white or pinkish
**Fruit:** 3-segmented capsules

Remarkably fleshy, succulent leaves make this species easily distinguishable. These juicy basal leaves completely encircle the stem to showcase the tiny, delicate flowers. • The common name comes from the fact that early settlers (and miners) indeed collected this plant for salads. The genus name *Claytonia* is in honor of John Clayton, an early botanist of note. **Where found:** moist, open to shady sites, often sandy soils; forests, thickets, meadows, disturbed sites; low to mid elevations (below 6000 ft). **Also known as:** *Montia perfoliata*.

# Threeleaf Lewisia

### *Lewisia triphylla*

**Height:** 1–4 in
**Leaves:** ⅜–2 in long, 2–3 paired or whorled
**Flowers:** ½ in wide, white or pinkish with darker veins
**Fruit:** capsules, ⅛ in long

Named *triphylla* (for 3 leaves), this plant most often only displays 2. There are no basal leaves, and the 2 upper, fleshy leaves are opposite each other and upward-pointing like a set of wings. The flowers have 5–9 petals and 3–5 stamens with colorful anthers. • This is a favored plant for rock gardens and is sometimes overcollected from the wild. • The genus *Lewisia* is named in honor of Captain Meriwether Lewis of the Lewis and Clark expeditions. **Where found:** moist, sandy sites, damp areas or on bare ground; Cascade and Coast ranges; 5000–11,000 ft.

185

# Field Chickweed

### *Cerastium arvense*

**Height:** 2–12 in
**Leaves:** ¹/₂–1¹/₄ in long, narrow
**Flowers:** ¹/₈–¹/₂ in wide, white, 5 deeply notched petals
**Fruit:** capsules, 2–3¹/₂ in long

These open, flat-topped clusters of cheerful flowers brighten stony slopes. • Aptly named, chickweed was fed to chickens, goslings and caged birds, especially when the birds were ill. • The genus name *Cerastium* comes from the Greek *kerastes*, "horned," in reference to the curved, cylindrical capsules, which open by 10 small teeth at the tip. The leaves of this loosely clumped perennial often have secondary, leafy tufts in their axils. **Where found:** dry, open, often rocky sites in plains to alpine zones.

# Seabluff Catchfly

### *Silene douglasii*

**Height:** 4–16 in
**Leaves:** ³/₄ to 3 in long, hairy
**Flowers:** petals ¹/₂ in long, white to greenish or pinkish, sepals ¹/₂ in long, fused in a chalice
**Fruit:** capsule, ³/₈–¹/₂ in long

The long, slender stem of seabluff catchfly is covered with tiny hairs and bears either a terminal flower or branches off into several stalks, each with a flower head. Usually several plants will grow in a clump, resembling erect bouquets of flowers above low, lush, green leaves. **Where found:** dry flats, gravelly sites, forest openings; low to mid elevations of the Coast and Cascade ranges. **Also known as:** Douglas' catchfly.

# American Winter Cress

### *Barbarea orthoceras*

**Height:** ¹/₂–2 ft
**Leaves:** to 4¹/₂ in long, becoming simpler and smaller higher up the stem
**Flowers:** ¹/₂ in long, yellow, 4-petaled, clustered in a raceme
**Fruit:** seedpods (siliques), to 2 in long

This biennial herb grows fairly tall and erect from its woody base and explodes in bright yellow flower clusters. The leaves are interesting and distinctive, with 2–3 pairs of smaller lobes and one large lobe. **Where found:** moist to wet forests and openings; meadows, streambanks, beaches; low to mid elevations.

# Field Mustard

### *Brassica rapa*

**Height:** 1–6 ft
**Leaves:** up to 12 in long, lobed, becoming simpler and smaller higher up the stem
**Flowers:** yellow, 4 petals, ½ in wide
**Fruit:** narrow pods, 1–2 in long

Golden fields of mustard in spring are a beautiful sight and often one of the first splashes of color announcing spring. Though there are many genera in the mustard family, the *Brassica* are the ones that most commonly come to mind. A member of a group of cultivated plants, *Brassica* is Latin for "cabbage" and *rapa* means "turnip." The word "mustard" appears to derive from the Latin *mustum* for "new wine," which was the first pressing of the grapes and was mixed with crushed mustard seeds to make a sauce. **Where found:** agricultural areas below 4000 ft. **Also known as:** rapeseed, *B. campestris.*

# Shepherd's Purse

### *Capsella bursa-pastoris*

**Height:** up to 20 in
**Leaves:** stem leaves 2½ in long, reduced in size upward; basal leaves to 2¼ in long
**Flowers:** <¼ in across, white
**Fruit:** flattened, triangular silicles, 2–3 in long

One of the telltale indicators that a flower belongs to the mustard family is the 4 petals in a symmetrical cross (the family was once called Cruciferae for "cross"). The flowers are usually numerous in a cluster at the top of the stem. • This introduced species can be invasive in cultivated fields but was used in Europe for centuries as a spice. **Where found:** waste areas and disturbed sites, roadsides, open, wild and cultivated fields, gardens; low to subalpine elevations. **Also known as:** pepper plant, pickpocket, witches'-pouches, toothwort, shovelplant.

# Peppergrass

### *Lepidium nitidum*

**Height:** 4–16 in
**Leaves:** opposite, alternating, becoming simpler and smaller higher up the stem
**Flowers:** ¼ in across
**Fruit:** oval seedpod, ¼ in long

Many mustards are more noticeable for their seedpods than for their flowers, and shiny peppergrass is no exception. When the tiny, white flowers go to seed, they drop their petals, and the seedpods mature from green to a gorgeous reddish purple. The seedpods give this species its common name because they are shiny and peppery-tasting. **Where found:** in large patches on dry flats, grassy slopes and disturbed sites below 3000 ft.

# California Poppy

### *Eschscholtzia californica*

**Height:** 2–24 in
**Leaves:** mostly basal, highly divided (parsley-like)
**Flowers:** solitary, yellow to orange, 4 petals, to 2 in wide
**Fruit:** pod-like capsules

The state flower of California, this bright and showy flower sets fields and slopes ablaze with orange and gold. There are many varieties of California poppy, but they all have a distinctive pink pedestal like a platter with the bloom showcased atop. This plant is more noticeable once the leaves fall and only the fat, dry seedpods remain. **Where found:** roadsides, clearings, dry rocky slopes; low elevations.

# Pacific Bleeding Heart

### *Dicentra formosa*

**Height:** 6–20 in
**Leaves:** 12 in long, basal, fern-like
**Flowers:** pink-purple, heart-shaped, ¾–1 in long
**Fruit:** small, oblong capsules

Native to North America and Asia, the common name refers to the heart-shaped flower, which ranges in color from light pink to intense deep purple or magenta. This plant is also cultivated and highly hybridized in color and size for gardens. The soft, leafy fern-like foliage is one of the common lush, green groundcovers in shady, moist forests. **Where found:** moist sites along ravines and streambanks and in forests; low to mid elevations. **Also known as:** western bleeding heart.

# Brook Saxifrage

### *Saxifraga odontoloma*

**Height:** ½–1½ ft
**Leaves:** up to 8 in long, basal, toothed
**Flowers:** ¼ in across, 5 petals
**Fruit:** capsules, ¼ in long

Saxifrage means "stone breaker," referring to the preference of some species for rocky habitats such as mountain ridges or even stone walls. • Brook saxifrage displays all the characteristics of a typical saxifrage: a leafless stem rising above large, round, basal, scallop-toothed leaves and many gracefully hanging flowers with spade-shaped white petals and contrasting yellow dots. **Where found:** wet meadows and along mountain streams in mid to high elevations.

# Small-flowered Woodland Star

### *Lithophragma parviflorum*

**Height:** 1–3 ft
**Leaves**: 1–2 in wide, 3-lobed, basal
**Flowers:** ½ in across, white to pink, 4–14 alternately arranged up the stem
**Fruit:** 3-chambered capsules

Caught up in a breeze, these star-like flowers atop their slender stems sway like magic wands conducting spells across the meadows. The white, pink or lavender flowers have 5 petals, each with 3 lobes, and are closely attached to the stems. • This flower makes its appearance in spring on wooded foothills where, typical of the saxifrage family, it finds its preferred rocky habitat. **Where found:** grassy slopes, open areas with rocky soil, dry forests, coastal bluffs; low to mid elevations.

# Foamflower

### *Tiarella trifoliata*

**Height:** to 20 in
**Leaves:** divided into 3 short-stemmed, coarsely toothed leaflets
**Flowers:** ⅛–¼ in across, in clusters on wiry stalks
**Fruit:** capsules

Delicate white flowers atop slender stems and broad, maple-like leaves characterize this abundant plant. This plant gets its name because the flowers look like flecks of foam. • When the fruits mature, the capsules split open to resemble sugar scoops and sprinkle out tiny, black seeds. **Where found:** abundant across the state; moist wood edges; Cascade and Coast ranges. **Also known as:** sugar scoop.

# Pacific Sedum

### *Sedum spathulifolium*

**Height:** 2–12 in
**Leaves:** ¾ in long, ⅜ in wide, basal
**Flowers:** ⅜ in long, yellow, in flat-topped clusters
**Fruit:** erect follicles in 5 segments

Stonecrops are noted for their distinctive succulent leaves, a strategy to conserve water in dry habitats. Pacific sedum has crowded, succulent, wedge-shaped leaves that alternate to form a basal rosette. These delicate leaves turn reddish if exposed to full sunshine; however, they remain green long after being picked, giving them the colloquial name "live-long." Starbursts of 5–50 bright yellow flowers top the leafy stems. **Where found:** shady to partially shady rocky sites or coarse soils, mountain cliffs, coastal bluffs, forest openings; low to mid elevations. **Also known as:** broad-leaved stonecrop.

# Windflower

### *Anemone drummondii*

**Height:** 4–10 in
**Leaves:** ³/₄–2 in long
**Flowers:** 1–1¹/₂ in wide
**Fruit:** achenes, <1 in long, in clusters

A burst of yellow stamens and 5–8 white or bluish sepals are the showy parts of this flower, which doesn't actually have true petals. After the flowers fade, the woolly, spherical fruits catch our interest, looking like wind-tousled heads and giving the plant its common name as well as the genus name *Anemone*, which means "shaken in the wind." • This plant thrives in windy, high-alpine conditions. **Where found:** rocky areas in mid to high elevations. **Also known as:** Drummond's anemone, alpine anemone.

# Western Columbine

### *Aquilegia formosa*

**Height:** 1–4 ft
**Leaves:** variable, usually twice divided into 3s, ³/₈–2 in long
**Flowers:** 1–1¹/₂ in long, tubular, red and yellow with reddish spurs
**Fruit:** 5 erect follicles with hairy, spreading tips

The Haida had a superstition that picking these flowers would bring on rain, while other Native groups considered the flower a good luck charm. • These nectar producers entice hummingbirds, butterflies and people to sip their sweet nectar, though the latter do a poor job at pollinating. The entire flower is edible and decorative in salads. **Where found:** moist, open to partly shady meadows, forests openings, clearings, rocky slopes, beaches; low elevation to treeline. **Also known as:** crimson columbine, red columbine.

# Marsh Marigold

### *Caltha leptosepala*

**Height:** 4–12 in
**Leaves:** to 2¹/₂ in long, 1–3 in wide, basal
**Flowers:** ³/₄–1¹/₂ in wide, white or greenish
**Fruit:** up to ³/₄ in long, beaked, bright yellow-green, in a cluster of 3–8

This species has a few distinctive, eye-catching characteristics that help to identify it. Marsh marigold has large, fleshy basal leaves, 5–10 or more showy, white sepals and many bright yellow-green stamens and pistils clumped in the center of the flower. • Native groups in Alaska enjoyed eating many parts of this species, yet for some reason, the plant was not so appreciated in our area. However, in Alaska the leaves and flowers were eaten raw or cooked, the long, white roots were boiled and the flower heads were pickled like capers. **Where found:** marshy sites in meadows or along streambanks. **Also known as:** alpine white marsh marigold.

# Western Buttercup

### *Ranunculus occidentalis*

**Height:** ½–2 ft
**Leaves:** variable, 1–4 in long
**Flowers:** ½–1 in wide, yellow
**Fruit:** spherical head of 5–20 tiny achenes

The butter analogy only goes as far as the color, not to any culinary uses—this plant is poisonous to people and livestock. However, buttercup essence is popular and is derived for use in holistic treatments. It is said to help the soul realize its inner light and beauty. • A Native legend tells of Coyote playing with his eyeballs and tossing them into the air. Eagle swooped down and snatched them, and Coyote had to make new eyes from buttercup flowers. **Where found:** damp meadows, grassy slopes, coastal bluffs, sagebrush scrub and forest openings.

# Meadowrue

### *Thalictrum* spp.

**Height:** 1–5 ft
**Leaves:** ½–2 in long, divided 3–4 times into 3s
**Flowers:** sepals <1 in, petals absent
**Fruit:** achenes, <1 in long

These tall, delicate woodland plants produce inconspicuous, greenish to purplish, male or female flowers without petals. The flowers have long sepals and either dangling anthers or greenish to purplish, lance-shaped fruits (achenes) in loose clusters, depending on the time of year. • The pleasant-smelling plants and seeds were burned in smudges or stored with possessions as insect repellent and perfume. Chewed seeds were rubbed onto hair and skin as perfume. **Where found:** moist sites in foothills, and montane and subalpine zones.

# Beach Strawberry

### *Fragaria chiloensis*

**Height:** to 10 in
**Leaves:** to 8 in, leathery, 3 leaflets
**Flowers:** to 1½ in wide, 5–7 petals
**Fruit:** strawberry, to ½ in wide

There are several species of strawberry in various habitats in our area, always distinguishable by the spreading runners, white flowers and, of course, sweet red fruits. This species of strawberry, however, is one of the parents of all cultivated strawberries (*F. virginiana* is another and looks very similar). • The fruits of beach strawberry can be made into jams, pies and other sweet treats, but they are tiny and take some patience to collect in quantity and self-control to not simply pop them into one's mouth! **Where found:** sand dunes, sea bluffs, beaches; sea level. **Also known as:** coastal strawberry.

191

# Redwood Sorrel

### *Oxalis oregana*

**Height:** 2–6 in
**Leaves:** 2–8 in long, basal, long-stalked
**Flowers:** ¹/₂–³/₄ in long, white to pinkish with reddish veins, 5 petals
**Fruit:** 5-chambered capsule, ¹/₄–³/₈ in long

The 3 heart-shaped leaflets of the leaves of redwood sorrel could be mistaken for those of clover. Sorrel leaves fold downward at night, in direct sunlight or in the rain but otherwise are held out horizontally. • This sour-tasting plant produces oxalic acid. Native groups did eat sorrel leaves, but they can be toxic in large quantities. **Where found:** moist sites, meadows and open forests; low to mid elevations.

# Wood Violet

### *Viola glabella*

**Height:** to 20 in
**Leaves:** to 2 in wide, heart-shaped
**Flowers:** ⁵/₈ in long, yellow
**Fruit:** capsules

Though this violet is yellow, violets can be various colors, from the typical violet-blue to white to yellow, often with violet-colored stripes on the lower 3 petals. • This violet species is very hardy, resistant to most diseases and also very prolific. A successful pioneer species in clearings and disturbed sites, it produces many brown seeds in explosive capsules and can populate available ground space quickly. **Where found:** moist forests, glades, clearings, streamsides; all elevations. **Also known as:** pioneer violet, yellow wood violet.

# Broadleaf Lupine

### *Lupinus polyphyllus*

**Height:** to 5 ft
**Leaves:** to 5 in long, with 10–17 leaflets
**Flowers:** ¹/₂ in long, in dense clusters 3–16 in long
**Fruit:** seedpods, to 2 in long

These attractive perennials, with their showy flower clusters and fuzzy seedpods, enrich the soil with nitrogen. • The pods look like hairy garden peas, and children may incorrectly assume that they are edible. Many lupines contain poisonous alkaloids, and it is difficult to distinguish between poisonous and non-poisonous species. • The leaves are silvery-hairy, and the pea-like flowers have silky upper sides. **Where found:** wet, open areas and disturbed sites; low to mid elevations.

# Clovers

### *Trifolium* spp.

**Height:** from 1–10 in depending on the species
**Leaves:** divided into 3 leaflets, variable in size depending on the species
**Flowers:** tiny, in dense flower heads
**Fruit:** pods, variable in size depending on the species

Clovers are one of the most familiar flowering plants, beloved for their promise of luck to those who find a "leaf of four." Although clovers are quickly identifiable, they can be quite diverse in color, ranging from white to bright fuchsia, and in size, varying from tiny species that hide in the grass to tall, proud species with lofty leaves. • The flower heads are a tight cluster of small flowers that are identifiable as members of the pea family (Fabaceae) for the banner, wings and hidden keel formations. **Where found:** various grassy habitats; low to subalpine elevations; often invasive.

# Winter Vetch

### *Vicia villosa*

**Height:** vine, 2–5 ft long
**Leaves:** hairy, divided into 5–10 pairs of narrow leaflets, each 1–2 in long, leaf tips with tendrils
**Flowers:** ¾ in long, in a long-stalked cluster of 10–40 flowers
**Fruit:** smooth pods, ½–¾ in long

An introduced annual or biennial, this vetch thrives in our climate. It is very hairy overall with often 2-toned flowers that combine reds or purples with white. East of the Cascades, its abundance is visible, with entire hillsides often tinted purple with these flowers. • Vetch flowers are longer than wide, differentiating them from lupine, wild pea and lotus flowers. **Where found:** disturbed sites; east of the Cascades. **Also known as:** woolly vetch.

# Fireweed

### *Epilobium angustifolium*

**Height:** 1–10 ft
**Leaves:** ¾–8 in, lance-shaped
**Flowers:** ¾–1⅝ in wide, in long, erect clusters
**Fruit:** narrow, pod-like capsules, 1⅝–3 in long

Fireweed helps heal landscape scars (e.g., roadsides, burned forests) by blanketing the ground with colonies of plants, often producing a sea of deep pink flowers. • Young shoots can be eaten like asparagus, and the flowers can be added to salads. • The erect pods split lengthwise to release hundreds of tiny seeds tipped with fluffy, white hairs. **Where found:** open, often disturbed sites in foothills to subalpine zones.

# Cow Parsnip

### *Heracleum lanatum*

**Height:** up to 10 ft
**Leaves:** 6–16 in long, divided into 3 large segments
**Flowers:** tiny, white, in large, flat-topped clusters up to 1 ft wide
**Fruit:** ¼–½ in long

The tiny flowers are in contrast to the overall largeness of this member of the carrot family (Apiaceae). Even its genus name derives from the great Hercules of Greek mythology. • Cow parsnip can cause skin irritation because it contains phototoxic furanocoumarins that are activated by exposure to sunlight. The plant is edible and was a valuable staple to many Native groups. Be careful not to confuse it with highly poisonous hemlock species that are similar in appearance. **Where found:** streambanks, moist slopes and clearings, upper beaches, marshes; sea level to subalpine elevations. **Also known as:** *H. sphondylium.*

# Northern Gentian

### *Gentianella amarella*

**Height:** 4–20 in
**Leaves:** 2 in long, in pairs
**Flowers:** <1 in long, bluish. tubular
**Fruit:** capsules

The flowers, about the width of a dime, have petals that range in color from blue to pink-violet to purple and that barely extend past the green sepals. The basal leaves are egg-shaped, form a cluster and fade early in the season, while the pairs of narrower stem leaves persist. • The genus name *Gentianella* means "little gentian," having been split off from the genus *Gentiana.* **Where found:** moist meadows and clearings, 5000–11,000 ft. **Also known as:** felwort.

# Western Waterleaf

### *Hydrophyllum occidentale*

**Height:** ½–2 ft
**Leaves:** divided into 7–15 segments, each 1½ in long
**Flowers:** tiny, lavender, bell-shaped, in clusters
**Fruit:** ovoid capsules, about ⅛– ¼ in wide with 1–3 seeds

The somewhat hairy, somewhat cupped leaves of this plant are adapted to collect and hold a bit of water, hence their namesake. • The dense inflorescence has a hairy appearance owing to the long stamens and pistils that reach out of the flowers by about ½ in. **Where found:** moist woods, forest openings; foothills to mid-mountain elevations mainly in Oregon.

# Baby Blue-eyes

### Nemophila menziesii

**Height:** 4–12 in
**Leaves:** 1–2 in long, deeply 5–13-lobed
**Flowers:** 1½ in across, bowl-shaped, blue with white center
**Fruit:** capsules, ¼–½ in wide

When scattered among the green grass of the foothills in spring, baby blue-eyes wink and capture your own eyes with their beauty. They are atypical of the waterleaf family (Hydrophyllaceae), lacking the fuzzy leaves or the long, protruding flower parts, but they do have the characteristic, slightly overlapping 5 petals. • The species name for this lovely flower honors 18th-century naturalist and explorer Archibald Menzies. **Where found:** grassy flats, meadows, forest openings and slopes; in the Cascades from 50–5000 ft, mainly in Oregon.

# Varileaf Phacelia

### Phacelia heterophylla

**Height:** up to 4 ft
**Leaves:** varying lengths diminishing up the stem
**Flowers:** ¼ in wide, white to greenish
**Fruit:** ovoid capsule, ⅛ in long

In spring, this entire plant has an overall fuzzy, green appearance, with the numerous flower heads appearing as tight green spheres. The flowers, which have long, protruding stamens, bloom in tight clusters that form an inflorescence that is reminiscent of either fuzzy caterpillars or coiled scorpion tails. The flower eventually fades to a rusty color, and the plant becomes inconspicuous. • The leaves of this plant vary in size and shape, giving it both its common name and the species name *heterophylla*, which is Greek for "varied leaf." **Where found:** open areas, exposed banks and foothills of the sagebrush ecosystem; mostly east of the Cascades.

# Spreading Phlox

### Phlox diffusa

**Height:** 2–4 in
**Leaves:** ¼–¾ in long, paired
**Flowers:** ½–¾ in wide, white, pink or bluish, solitary
**Fruit:** 3-chambered capsule

This phlox gets its name for its beautiful way of pouring over rocks in low, loose mats that carpet the ground with dense greenery or, when in bloom, blankets of brightly colored flowers. Each sweet-smelling blossom is a pinwheel-like fan of 5 petals fused at their bases into a tube ⅜–⅝ in long. **Where found:** open, rocky outcrops, slopes and scree, open forests; low montane to above treeline.

# Pennyroyal

### *Monardella odoratissima*

**Height:** 1¹⁄₂–2 ft
**Leaves:** ¹⁄₄–1³⁄₄ in long, in pairs
**Flowers:** ³⁄₈–¹⁄₂ in long, whitish to pale purple or pink, in terminal clusters
**Fruit:** oblong nutlets

This plant's strong scent will leave no doubt that this is a mint, and its flavor is so strong that even cold water will become infused. In addition, the square stem is a telltale characteristic of members of the mint family (Lamiaceae). • The flower heads are composed of many small flowers with long bracts and protruding stamens, and these plants typically grow in crowded masses, filling areas with color and fragrance. **Where found:** dry slopes and sagebrush scrub, montane forests; Coast and Cascade ranges. **Also known as:** mountain monardella, coyote mint.

# Bedstraw

### *Galium boreale*

**Height:** 8–15¹⁄₂ in
**Leaves:** ³⁄₄–2¹⁄₂ in long, 3-veined, in whorls of 4
**Flowers:** ¹⁄₈–¹⁄₄ in across, creamy white, in terminal clusters
**Fruit:** nutlets, <¹⁄₈ in across

Bedstraws are related to coffee, and their tiny, paired, short-hairy nutlets can be dried, roasted and ground to make a coffee substitute. • Bedstraw juice or tea was applied to many skin problems. Some people take the tea to speed weight loss, but continual use irritates the mouth, and people with poor circulation or diabetes should not use it. • The flowers grow in repeatedly 3-forked clusters. • Sweet-scented bedstraw (*G. triflorum*) has whorls of 6 broader, bristle-tipped leaves, and its nutlets are covered with long, hooked bristles. **Where found:** open sites and roadsides; mountain forests to subalpine zones; Olympic Mountains.

# Scarlet Paintbrush

### *Castilleja miniata*

**Height:** 8–24 in
**Leaves:** 2–2³⁄₄ in long
**Flowers:** ³⁄₄ –1¹⁄₄ in long, greenish, tubular, concealed by hairy, red bracts
**Fruit:** 2-celled capsules

It is usually easy to recognize a paintbrush, but *Castilleja* is a confusing genus, with many flower shapes and colors and species that often hybridize. • Paintbrushes have reduced photosynthetic abilities and partially parasitize nearby plants to steal nutrients. • Showy, leaf-like bracts give these flower clusters their red color. The actual flowers are the tubular, greenish blossoms concealed within the bracts. **Where found:** open woods and meadows, grassy slopes, tidal marshes, disturbed sites; foothills and montane zones. **Also known as:** common red paintbrush, giant paintbrush, great red paintbrush.

# Yellow Monkeyflower

## *Mimulus guttatus*

**Height:** 4–20 in
**Leaves:** ¹/₂–2 in long, in pairs
**Flowers:** ¹/₂–1⁵/₈ in long, yellow, trumpet-shaped
**Fruit:** oblong capsules, ¹/₂–³/₄ in long

These snapdragons brighten streamsides, rocky seeps and wet ditches.
• *Mimulus* is the diminutive form of the Latin *mimus*, meaning "a buffoon or actor in a farce or mime." The common name also alludes to the fancied resemblance of these flowers to small, grinning, ape-like faces.
• This variable species often roots from nodes or sends out stolons.
**Where found:** wet sites in foothills and montane and subalpine zones.
**Also known as:** seep monkeyflower.

# Davidson's Penstemon

## *Penstemon davidsonii*

**Height:** 4–6 in
**Leaves:** ¹/₄–⁵/₈ in, mat-forming
**Flowers:** 1–2 in long, tubular
**Fruit:** narrowly winged capsules, ¹/₃ in long

The richly purple to lavender blue flowers are relatively large compared to the small evergreen leaves and low growth form of this plant. The 5 petals unite into long, 2-lipped tubes that stand out like loud purple trumpets among the drab-colored rocks that are this plant's preferred habitat. The throats and anthers of the flowers are woolly, adding to the interest of these showy flowers. **Where found:** rocky ridges near and above treeline in the Cascades. **Also known as:** alpine penstemon.

# American Brooklime

## *Veronica americana*

**Height:** 4–27¹/₂ in
**Leaves:** to 2 in long
**Flowers:** ¹/₄ in wide, saucer-shaped
**Fruit:** round capsules, ¹/₈ in long

The leaves of American brooklime are edible and commonly used in salads or as a potherb. Because this plant most often grows directly in water, be sure not to collect the leaves from plants in polluted sites.
• The showy flowers are blue to violet, sometimes white, with red-purple markings and 2 large, reaching stamens that look like antennae.
**Where found:** shallow water alongside slow-moving streams, springs, marshes, seepage areas, wet meadows, clearings and ditches; low to mid elevations. **Also known as:** American speedwell.

# Twinflower

### *Linnaea borealis*

**Height:** 1¼–4 in, trailing
**Leaves:** ½–¾ in long, opposite
**Flowers:** ¼–⅝ in long, pink, trumpet-like
**Fruit:** nutlets, <⅛ in across, with sticky hairs

The small, delicate pairs of nodding bells are easily over-looked among other plants on the forest floor, but their strong, sweet perfume may draw you to them in the evening. • Hooked bristles on the tiny, egg-shaped nutlets catch on the fur, feathers or clothing of passersby, who then carry these inconspicuous hitchhikers to new locations. • This trailing, semi-woody ever-green is an excellent native groundcover in partially shaded sites. **Where found:** moist, open or dense shaded forests, shrub thickets, muskeg, rocky shorelines; from foothills to subalpine zones.

# Common Yarrow

### *Achillea millefolium*

**Height:** 4–31 in
**Leaves:** 1¼–4 in long, fern-like
**Flowers:** <¼ in wide, white or pinkish with cream-colored centers, in clusters
**Fruit:** hairless, flattened achenes

This hardy, aromatic perennial has served for thousands of years as a fumigant, insecticide and medicine. The Greek hero Achilles, for whom the genus was named, supposedly used it to heal his soldiers' wounds after battle. • Yarrow is also an attractive ornamental, but beware—its extensive underground stems (rhizomes) can soon invade your garden. **Where found:** dry to moist, open sites from plains to alpine zones.

# Leafy Aster

### *Symphyotrichum foliaceum* var. *foliaceum*

**Height:** ½–3 ft
**Leaves:** 2–6 in
**Flowers:** ray flowers ⅓–¾ in long; disk flowers tiny, yellow
**Fruit:** hairy achenes

One of the loveliest flowers in our area is also one of the most com-mon. The yellow disk flowers in the center of the inflorescence are surrounded by ray flowers that can range in color from white to blue to pink, purple or red. Directly below the inflorescence is a collar of many green, leafy bracts that stick out perpendicular to the stem. **Where found:** open woods, meadows, streambanks; throughout the Sierras; mid to high elevations (5000–8000 ft). **Also known as:** leafy-headed aster, *Aster foliaceus*.

# Brass Buttons

## *Cotula coronopifolia*

**Height:** 8–16 in
**Leaves:** 3/8–1 3/8 in long, narrow
**Flowers:** 1/4–1/2 in wide, yellow, rays absent
**Fruit:** achenes

True to their name, the showy, bright yellow, disk-shaped flower heads of this plant look like shiny brass buttons, and they are also pleasantly aromatic. • Brass buttons is a South African species introduced to our area, as well as to many other parts of the world, where it typically colonizes beaches, reminding many people of home when they are on a beach vacation. They are very salt tolerant but also brighten up brackish, muddy, non-coastal sites. **Where found:** beaches, tidal mudflats, marshes, salt marshes, estuaries; along the coast and near inland vernal pools. **Also known as:** mud disk, golden buttons, buttonweed.

# Subalpine Fleabane

## *Erigeron peregrinus*

**Height:** 4–28 in
**Leaves:** 1/2–8 in long
**Flowers:** ray flowers 30–80, pink or purplish; disk yellow; in heads 3/4–2 1/2 in wide
**Fruit:** hairy, ribbed achenes with hair-like parachutes

These star-like flower heads often appear in Native basketry patterns. • Fleabanes, a type of daisy, are easily confused with asters. Aster flower heads usually have overlapping rows of bracts with light, parchment-like bases and green tips. Fleabanes usually have 1 row of slender bracts with the same texture and color (not green) throughout. Also, fleabanes generally flower earlier and have narrower, more numerous rays. **Where found:** moist to wet, open sites in foothills to alpine zones. **Also known as:** subalpine daisy.

# Common Tarweed

## *Madia elegans*

**Height:** 1–3 ft
**Leaves:** 3/4–8 in long
**Flowers:** ray flowers 3/8–5/8 in long, yellow; disk flowers yellow; in heads 1–1 1/2 in wide
**Fruit:** achenes

The long, golden ray flowers are often 2-toned, with either white or a dark red to maroon color at the bases. • The name "tarweed" refers to the plant's sticky, black glandular hairs, which readily stick to skin and clothing upon contact. The fragrance of tarweed is also heavy and sticky, almost tar-like. • The flowers close at midday but remain open throughout the rest of the day as well as through the evening. **Where found:** grassy fields below 3000 ft in Oregon. **Also known as:** common madia, elegant tarweed.

# Woolly Mule Ears

## *Wyethia mollis*

**Height:** 10–20 in
**Leaves:** 8–16 in long, gray-green, mostly basal
**Flowers:** ray flowers 5–20, yellow, disk flowers yellow, in heads up to 4 in wide
**Fruit:** achenes, ³/₈ in long

Large masses of woolly mule ears often cover mid-elevation meadows, telling you that the hillside they are growing on is almost definitely of volcanic origin. The long roots of this species can reach deep into the porous volcanic soil to find water that other plants cannot access. • The name "mule ears" refers to this plant's relatively large leaves, which grow vertically upward. The plant's dense woolly hairs and leaf growth formation help reduce water loss. **Where found:** open slopes at 4000–10,500 ft in the Cascade Range of southeastern Oregon. **Also known as:** narrow-leaved mule ears.

# Heart-leaved Arnica

## *Arnica cordifolia*

**Height:** 4–24 in
**Leaves:** 1⅝–4 in, basal, long-stemmed
**Flowers:** in heads 1–2½ in wide
**Fruit:** achene, ¼–³/₈ in long

Some Native groups used these yellow wildflowers in love charms because of their heart-shaped leaves. Rootstocks and flowers were used in washes and poultices for treating bruises, sprains and swollen feet, but these poisonous plants should never be applied to broken skin. • This single-stemmed perennial produces seed-like fruits with tufts of white, hair-like bristles. **Where found:** open woods and slopes in submontane to subalpine zones.

# Sitka Valerian

## *Valeriana sitchensis*

**Height:** 1–3½ ft
**Leaves:** to 10 in long, in pairs on the stem, each divided into 3–7 leaflets
**Flowers:** ⅛–¼ in long, white to pale pink
**Fruit:** egg-shaped, ribbed achenes, ⅛–¼ in long

If the delicate flower clusters of this plant don't catch your attention, the odor may. Dried, frozen or bruised plants have a strong, unpleasant smell. • The stems are 4-sided, and the seed-like fruits are tipped with feathery hairs. • This perennial was widely used as a sedative. The tranquilizer and muscle relaxant diazepam (Valium) was first extracted from valerian. **Where found:** moist to wet sites in foothills to subalpine zones; from northern Canada to Idaho and Montana.

# Bracken Fern

### *Pteridium aquilinum*

**Height:** fronds to 10 ft or taller
**Leaves:** blades triangular, 10 or more leaflets

This widespread species is common around the world and occurs in a wide variety of habitats, though in our area, it prefers open or disturbed sites. • The deep rhizomes spread easily and help the plant survive fires. • Native groups used the fronds to line pit ovens and ate the rhizomes. **Where found:** meadows, disturbed sites, clearings; dry to wet forests, lakeshores, bogs; low to subalpine elevations.

# Sword Fern

### *Polystichum munitum*

**Height:** up to 5 ft
**Leaves:** blades lance-shaped, many leaflets

Plants in the genus *Polystichum* are all large, tufted, evergreen ferns that form crown-like bunches from a single woody rhizome. The sword fern is one of several *Polystichum* species in our area. • This plant was used by Native groups for lining pit ovens, wrapping and storing food, flooring and bedding. • These ferns have large, circular sori (groups of spore sacs on the undersides of the leaflets). **Where found:** moist forests; low to mid elevations.

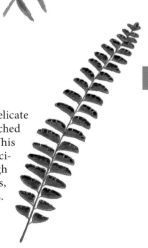

# Maidenhair Fern

### *Adiantum pedatum*

**Height:** 6–24 in
**Leaves:** palmate, many leaflets

Though it grows in colonies and can appear lush, this delicate fern typically has a single or very few palmately branched leaves on thin, dark brown or purple-black stems. • This fern was often used in Native basketry as well as medicinally. It was exported to Europe and used in herbal cough medicines. **Where found:** shady, humus-rich sites; forests, alongside streams and waterfalls; low to mid elevations.
**Also known as:** *A. aleuticum.*

# Surf Grass

### *Phyllospadix* spp.

**Length:** 3 ft

Not algae, not grass, but a type of flowering plant, surf grass is the only flowering plant that is truly marine. It spends almost its entire life underwater, rarely exposed at low tide, when long, narrow, bright green strands can be seen in shallow, rocky waters. • Sea grass flowers are tiny and inconspicuous because there is no need to attract insects for pollination. Pollen is released in long, thread-like strands and carried by water currents. The seeds are dispersed by water or fish. **Where found:** rocky coasts exposed to wave action.

# Turkish Towel · Red Algae

### *Gigartina exasperata*

**Length:** up to 6 ft

Most marine plants are algae—lacking flowers, leaves or roots. There are 3 types of algae along California's coast: green, brown and red. Turkish towel is among the most massive of red algae species. Red algae are the largest group of seaweeds. They are the most abundant and comprise most species of seaweed in the world. Two of the most notable along the California coast include nori (*Porphyra* spp., cultivated in East Asia and routinely used in Japanese cooking) and Turkish towel. • A red pigment typically masks the chlorophyll that would otherwise render these algae green in color. **Where found:** intertidal and low, subtidal zones.

# Giant Kelp · Brown Algae

### *Macrocystis* spp.

**Length:** up to 330 ft

*Macrocystis pyrifera* is the most admired brown algae and is the foundation for the entire marine ecosystem. It is particularly suited to the cold Pacific waters. • Giant kelp is the largest and fastest growing plant in the marine environment. The entire frond is able to photosynthesize and, under ideal conditions, this plant can grow up to 2 ft in a single day. • Kelp forests are among the most biodiverse forests, including terrestrial ones, in the world. **Where found:** in waters 50–68°F, on rocky substrate where the plant can attach.

# Bull Kelp · Brown Algae

### *Nereocystis luetkeana*

**Length:** 30–60 ft; up to 115 ft

Bull kelp forests provide habitat and shelter for a myriad of marine life—sea otters wrap themselves up in bull kelp that is adhered to the ocean floor so that they can take a nap without drifting away. • Bull kelp is hollow with a bulbous float at the top and is filled with gasses that are 10% carbon monoxide. **Where found:** attached to rocky substrates; populations are increasingly abundant north of San Francisco Bay.

# Sea Lettuce · Green Algae

### *Ulva lactuca*

**Length:** 7 in

There are few green algae species found in the intertidal zone, but the most visible and abundant is the bright green sea lettuce, which either attaches to rocks or is free-floating. • This algae has a very simple structure that is only 2 cells thick. • Sea lettuce has a high caloric value and is eaten by crabs and mollusks. **Where found:** shallow bays, lagoons, harbors and marshes; on rocks and on other algae in intertidal and high-tide zones.

# GLOSSARY

## A

**achene:** a seed-like fruit, e.g., sunflower seed

**alcids:** a family of birds that includes puffins, murrelets, auklets and other similar birds

**algae:** simple photosynthetic aquatic plants lacking true stems, roots, leaves and flowers, and ranging in size from single-celled forms to giant kelp

**altricial:** animals that are helpless at birth or hatching

**ammocetes:** larval lamprey

**anadromous:** fish that migrate from salt water to fresh water to spawn

**annual:** plants that live for only 1 year or growing season

**anterior:** situated at or toward the front

**aquatic:** water frequenting

**arboreal:** tree frequenting

**autotrophic:** an organism that produces its own food, e.g., by photosynthesis

## B

**barbels:** fleshy, whisker-like appendages found on some fish

**basal leaf:** a leaf arising from the base of a plant

**benthic:** bottom feeding

**berry:** a fleshy fruit, usually with several to many seeds

**bivalve:** a group of mollusks in which the animal is enclosed by 2 valves (shells)

**bract:** a leaf-like structure arising from the base of a flower or inflorescence

**bracteole:** a small bract borne on a leaf stalk

**brood parasite:** a bird that parasitizes other bird's nests by laying its eggs and then abandoning them for the parasitized birds to raise, e.g., brown-headed cowbird

**bulb:** a fleshy underground organ with overlapping, swollen scales, e.g., an onion

## C

**calyx:** a collective term for the sepals of a flower

**cambium:** inner layers of tissue that transport nutrients up and down the plant stalk or trunk

**canopy:** the fairly continuous cover provided by the branches and leaves of adjacent trees

**capsules:** a dry fruit that splits open to release seeds

**carapace:** a protective bony shell (e.g., of a turtle) or exoskeleton (e.g., of beetles)

**carnivorous:** feeding primarily on meat

**carrion:** decomposing animal matter; a carcass

**catkin:** a spike of small flowers

**chelipeds:** the clawed first pair of legs, e.g., on a crab

**compound leaf:** a leaf separated into 2 or more divisions called leaflets

**cone:** the fruit produced by a coniferous plant, composed of overlapping scales around a central axis

**coniferous:** cone-bearing; seed (female) and pollen (male) cones are borne on the same tree in different locations

**corm:** a swollen underground stem base used by some plants as an organ of propagation; resembles a bulb

**crepuscular:** active primarily at dusk and dawn

**cryptic coloration:** a coloration pattern designed to conceal an animal

# D

**deciduous:** a tree whose leaves turn color and are shed annually

**defoliating:** dropping of the leaves

**disk flower:** a small flower in the center, or disk, of a composite flower (e.g., aster, daisy or sunflower)

**diurnal:** active primarily during the day

**dorsal:** the top or back

**drupe:** a fleshy fruit with a stony pit, e.g., peach, cherry

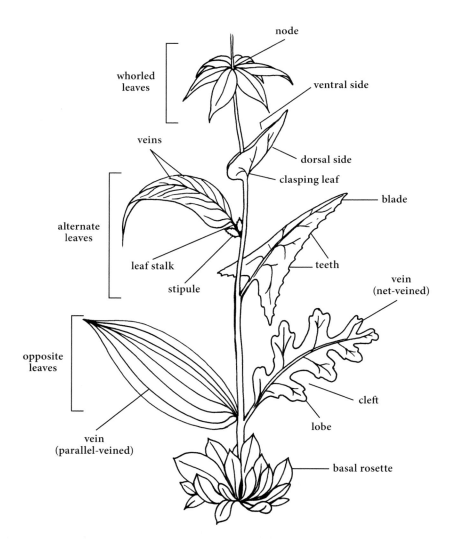

# E

**echolocation:** navigation by rebounding sound waves off objects to target or avoid them

**ecological niche:** an ecological role filled by a species

**ecoregion:** distinction between regions based upon geology, climate, biodiversity, elevation and soil composition

**ectoparasites:** skin parasites

**ectotherm:** an animal that regulates its body temperature behaviorally from external sources of heat, i.e., from the sun

**eft:** the stage of a newt's life following the tadpole stage, in which it exits the water and leads a terrestrial life; when the newt matures to adulthood it returns to the water

**endotherm:** an animal that regulates its body temperature internally

**estivate:** a state of inactivity and a slowing of the metabolism to permit survival in extended periods of high temperatures and inadequate water supply

**estuarine:** an area where a freshwater river exits into the sea; the salinity of the seawater drops because it is diluted by the fresh water

**eutrophic:** a nutrient-rich body of water with an abundance of algae growth and a low level of dissolved oxygen

**evergreen:** having green leaves through winter; not deciduous

**exoskeleton:** a hard outer encasement that provides protection and points of attachment for muscles

# F

**flight membrane:** the membrane between the fore and hind limbs of bats and some squirrels that allows bats to fly and squirrels to glide through the air

**follicle:** the structure in the skin from which hair or feathers grow; a dry fruit that splits open along a single line on one side when ripe; a cocoon

**food web:** the elaborated, interconnected feeding relationships of living organisms in an ecosystem

**forb:** a broad-leaved plant that lacks a permanent woody stem and loses its aboveground growth each year; may be annual, biennial or perennial

# G

**gillrakers:** long, thin, fleshy projections that protect delicate gill tissue from particles in the water

**glandular:** similar to or containing glands

## H

**habitat:** the physical area in which an organism lives

**hawking:** feeding behavior in which a bird leaves a perch, snatches its prey in midair, and then returns to its previous perch

**herbaceous:** feeding primarily on vegetation

**hibernation:** a state of decreased metabolism and body temperature and slowed heart and respiratory rates to permit survival during long periods of cold temperature and diminished food supply

**hibernaculum:** a shelter in which an animal, usually a mammal, reptile or insect, chooses to hibernate

**hind:** female elk (this term is used mostly in Asia—in North America "cow" is more often used)

**hips:** the berry-like fruit of some plants in the rose family (Rosaceae)

**holdfast:** the root-like structure that seaweeds use to hold onto rocky substrates

**hybrids:** the offspring from a cross between parents belonging to different varieties or subspecies, sometimes between different subspecies or genera

## I

**incubate:** to keep eggs at a relatively constant temperature until they hatch

**inflorescence:** a cluster of flowers on a stalk; may be arranged as a spike, raceme, head, panicle, etc.

**insectivorous:** feeding primarily on insects

**intertidal zone:** the area between low- and high-tide lines

**invertebrate:** any animal lacking a backbone, e.g., worms, slugs, crayfish, shrimps

**involucral bract:** one of several bracts that form a whorl below a flower or flower cluster

## K

**key:** a winged fruit, usually of an ash or maple; also called a "samara"

## L

**larva:** immature forms of an animal that differ from the adult

**leaflet:** a division of a compound leaf

**lenticel:** a slightly raised portion of bark where the cells are packed more loosely, allowing for gas exchange with the atmosphere

**lobate:** having each toe individually webbed

**lobe:** a projecting part of a leaf or flower, usually rounded

## M

**metabolic rate:** the rate of chemical processes in an organism

**metamorphosis:** the developmental transformation of an animal from larval to sexually mature adult stage

**midden:** the pile of cone scales found on the territories of tree squirrels, usually under a favorite tree

**molt:** when an animal sheds old feathers, fur or skin, in order to replace them with new growth

**montane:** of mountainous regions

**myccorhizal fungi:** fungi that has a mutually beneficial relationship with the roots of some seed plants

## N

**neotropical migrant:** a bird that nests in North America, but overwinters in the New World tropics

**nocturnal:** active primarily at night

**node:** a slightly enlarged section of a stem where leaves or branches originate

**nudibranch:** sea slug

**nutlet:** a small, hard, single-seeded fruit that remains closed

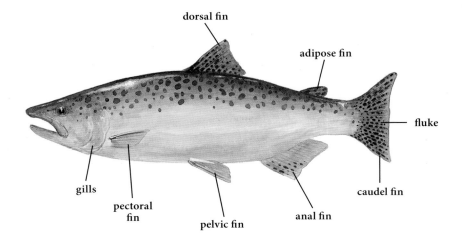

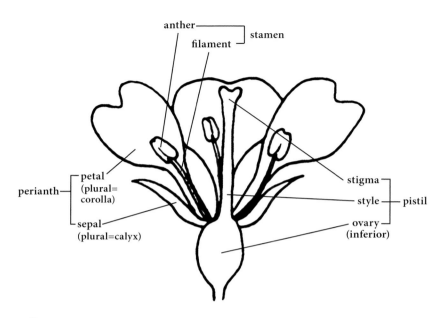

## O

**omnivorous:** feeding on both plants and animals

**ovoid:** egg-shaped

## P

**palmate:** leaflets, lobes or veins arranged around a single point, like the fingers on a hand (e.g., maple leaf)

**pappus:** the modified calyx of composite flowers (e.g., asters or daisies), consisting of awns, scales or bristles at the apex of the achene

**parasite:** a relationship between 2 species in which one benefits at the expense of the other

**patagium:** skin forming a flight membrane

**pelage:** the fur or hair of mammals

**perennial:** a plant that lives for several years

**petal:** a member of the inside ring of modified flower leaves, usually brightly colored or white

**phenology:** stages of growth as influenced by climate

**photosynthesis:** conversion of $CO_2$ and water into sugars via energy of the sun

**pinniped:** a marine mammal with limbs that are modified to form flippers; a seal, sea-lion or walrus

**pioneer species:** a plant species that is capable of colonizing an otherwise unvegetated area; one of the first species to take hold in a disturbed area

**piscivorous:** fish-eating

**pishing:** a noise made to attract birds

**pistil:** the female organ of a flower, usually consisting of an ovary, style and stigma

**plastic species:** a species that can adapt to a wide range of conditions

**plastron:** the lower part of a turtle or tortoise shell, which covers the abdomen

**poikilothermic:** having a body temperature that is the same as the external environment and varies with it

**pollen:** the tiny grains produced in a plant's anthers and which contain the male reproductive cells

**pollen cone:** male cone that produces pollen

**polyandry:** a mating strategy in which one female mates with several males

**pome:** a fruit with a core, e.g., apple

**precocial:** animals who are active and independent at birth or hatching

**prehensile:** able to grasp

**proboscis:** the elongated tubular and flexible mouthpart of many insects

# R

**ray flower:** in a composite flower (e.g., aster, daisy or sunflower), a type of flower usually with long, colorful petals that collectively make up the outer ring of petals (the center of a composite flower is composed of disk flowers)

**redd:** spawning nest for fish

**resinous:** bearing resin, usually causing stickiness

**rhinopores:** tentacle-like sensory structures on the head of a nudibranch (sea slug)

**rhizome:** a horizontal underground stem

**rictal bristles:** hair-like feathers found on the faces of some birds

**riparian:** on the bank of a river or other watercourse

**rookery:** a colony of nests

**runner:** a slender stolon or prostrate stem that roots at the nodes or the tip

# S

**samara:** a dry, winged fruit with usually only a single seed (e.g., maple or ash); also called a "key"

**salmonid:** a member of the Salmonidae family of fishes; includes trout, char, salmon, whitefish and grayling

**scutes:** individual plates on a turtle's shell

**seed cone:** female cone that produces seeds

**sepals:** the outer, usually green, leaf-like structures that protect the flower bud and are located at the base of an open flower

**silicle:** a fruit of the mustard family (Brassicaceae) that is 2-celled and usually short, wide and often flat

**silique:** a long, thin fruit with many seeds; characteristic of some members of the mustard family (Brassicaceae)

**sorus (pl. sori):** a collection of sporangia under a fern frond; in some lichens and fungi, a structure that produces pores

**spadix:** a fleshy spike with many small flowers

**spathe:** a leaf-like sheath that surrounds a spadix

**spur:** a pointed projection

**stamen:** the pollen-bearing organ of a flower

**stigma:** a receptive tip in a flower that receives pollen

**stolon:** a long branch or stem that runs along the ground and often propagates more plants

**subnivean:** below the surface of the snow

**substrate:** the surface that an organism grows on; the material that makes up a streambed (e.g., sand or gravel)

**suckering:** a method of tree and shrub reproduction in which shoots arise from an underground stem

**syrinx:** a bird's vocal organ

# T

**taproot:** the main, large root of a plant from which smaller roots arise, e.g., carrot

**tendril:** a slender, clasping or twining outgrowth from a stem or a leaf

**terrestrial:** land frequenting

**torpor:** a state of physical inactivity

**tragus:** a prominent structure of the outer ear of a bat

**tubercule:** a round nodule or warty outgrowth

**tubular flower:** a type of flower in which all or some of the petals are fused together at the base

**tundra:** a high-altitude ecological zone at the northernmost limits of plant growth, where plants are reduced to shrubby or mat-like growth

**tympanum:** eardrum; the hearing organ of a frog or lizard

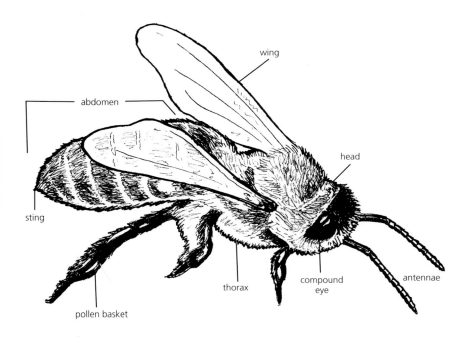

## U

**ungulate:** an animal that has hooves

## V

**ventral:** of or on the abdomen (belly)

**vermiculations:** wavy-patterned makings

**vertebrate:** an animal possessing a backbone

**vibrissae:** bristle-like feathers growing around the beak of birds to aid in catching insects

## W

**whorl:** a circle of leaves or flowers around a stem

**woolly:** bearing long or matted hairs

# REFERENCES

Acorn, John, and Ian Sheldon. 2002. *Bugs of Washington and Oregon*. Lone Pine Publishing, Edmonton, AB.

Bailey, Robert G. 1995. 2nd edition. *Descriptions of the Ecoregions of the United States*. USDA Forest Service, Washington, D.C. http://www.fs.fed.us/rm/analytics/publications/ecoregionsindex.html and http://www.fs.fed.us/rm/analytics/staff/Bailey.html. Accessed September 2007.

Bell, Brian H., and Gregory Kennedy. 2006. *Birds of Washington State*. Lone Pine Publishing, Edmonton, AB.

Bezener, Andy, and Linda Kershaw. 1999. *Rocky Mountain Nature Guide*. Lone Pine Publishing, Edmonton, AB.

Burrows, Roger, and Jeff Gilligan. 2003. *Birds of Oregon*. Lone Pine Publishing, Edmonton, AB.

Eder, Tamara. 2002. *Mammals of Washington and Oregon*. Lone Pine Publishing, Edmonton, AB.

Eder, Tamara. 2001. *Whales and other Marine Mammals of Washington and Oregon*. Lone Pine Publishing, Edmonton, AB.

Leatherwood, Stephen, and Randall R. Reeves. 1983. *The Sierra Club Handbook of Whales and Dolphins*. Sierra Club Books, San Francisco.

Lesher, Robin D., and Richard H. McClure Jr. 1986. *Major Indicator Shrubs and Herbs on National Forests of Western Oregon and Southwestern Washington*. USDA Forest Service Pacific Northwest Region, Portland, OR. http://www.reo.gov/ecoshare/publications/searchresults.asp. Accessed September 2007.

Lyons, C.P. 1999. *Trees & Shrubs of Washington*. Lone Pine Publishing, Edmonton, AB.

Lyons, C.P. 1997. *Wildflowers of Washington*. Lone Pine Publishing, Edmonton, AB.

*National Audubon Society Field Guide to North American Fishes, Whales & Dolphins*. 1998. Chanticleer Press, Toronto.

*National Audubon Society Field Guide to North American Seashore Creatures*. 1998. Chanticleer Press, Toronto.

Pojar, Jim, and Andy MacKinnon. 1994. *Plants of the Pacific Northwest Coast: Washington, Oregon, British Columbia & Alaska*. BC Ministry of Forests and Lone Pine Publishing, Edmonton, AB.

Sheldon, Ian. 1997. *Animal Tracks of Washington and Oregon*. Lone Pine Publishing, Edmonton, AB.

Sheldon, Ian. 1998. *Seashore of the Pacific Northwest*. Lone Pine Publishing, Edmonton, AB.

St. John, Alan. 2002. *Reptiles of the Northwest: California to Alaska, Rockies to the Coast*. Lone Pine Publishing, Edmonton, AB.

# INDEX

Names in **boldface** type indicate primary species.

# ABOUT THE AUTHOR

 Erin McCloskey spent her formative years observing nature from atop her horse. She received her BSc with distinction in environmental and conservation sciences, majoring in conservation biology and management. An active campaigner for the protection of endangered species and spaces, Erin has collaborated with various NGOs and has been involved in numerous conservation projects around the world. Currently, she is the North American operations manager for Biosphere Expeditions, located in Los Angeles. Erin began working as an editor with Lone Pine Publishing in 1996. From 2000–05, she lived in Italy, where she freelanced as a writer and editor; she was managing editor for *AK: Journal of Applied Kinesiology* and helped prepare scientific articles for several medical research institutions. She also worked as an editor for several publishers focused on nature and travel. Erin is the author of *The Bradt Travel Guide to Argentina, Ireland Flying High, Canada Flying High, Hawaii From the Air* and co-author for the *Green Volunteers* guidebook series. She is also the author of the *Northern California Nature Guide* for Lone Pine Publishing.